Sir Henry Wellcome
Backwood to Knighthood

John A. Flannery

Karen M. Smith

BOSTON SPA MEDIA

Authors and Editors: John A. Flannery, Karen M. Smith

Layout & pre-press: Boston Spa Media, Leeds, U.K.

Produced by: Boston Spa Media, Leeds, U.K.
www.bostonspamedia.com

Published by Boston Spa Media

Boston Spa Media
108, High Street
Boston Spa
Leeds
LS23 6DR
England
UK

Tel.: +44 (0)1937 849252
E-mail: enquiries@bostonspamedia.com

Press department: enquiries@bostonspamedia.com

www.bostonspamedia.com

ISBN 10:
0956591604

ISBN 13:
978-0-9565916-0-9

Copyright © 2011 Boston Spa Media

Printed in Europe by Beamreach Printing
www.beamreachuk.co.uk

Acknowledgements

In 2007 the Wellcome Library was refurbished to its former splendour and featured in our book, Library Design. Following this publication, we were invited to assess the possibilities for a new book featuring the images contained in the Wellcome Collection. From this vast archive, the pictorial story of Sir Henry Wellcome at first emerged, and then demanded to be told. The images contained in this book represent 160 years of photography, from the earliest Wellcome family portraits taken in the 1850s, to the Scanning Electron Microscope images featured in the chapter headings. For the invitation to work with this remarkable material we must thank Frances Norton, the former Head of the Wellcome Library, and the Chairman of the Wellcome Trust, Sir William Castell, who has kindly written the foreword for Backwood to Knighthood. We would also like to acknowledge the help of Clare Matterson, Ross MacFarlane and Simon Chaplin at the Wellcome Trust, and in particular Catherine Draycott and her willing staff at the Wellcome Images.

John A. Flannery

Karen M. Smith

Mr. J. A. Flannery is an author and Construction Consultant with qualifications in industrial design from Leeds Metropolitan University. John Flannery has over 30 years experience in the Design, Procurement and Project Management of a wide range of construction projects in the industrial, commercial and private sectors throughout Europe, Africa and the U.S.A. Mr. Flannery currently specialises in authoring books on ecological urban regeneration.

Karen Smith has a dual role as an Information Specialist and Academic Liaison Librarian at the University of York. Her extensive and varied career has encompassed both Public, University and Health Care Libraries. Currently Ms. Smith is based in the Department of Health Sciences and provides consultancy and lecturing on evidence-based practice and the effective use of information resources.

Sir Henry Wellcome

Backwood to Knighthood

Commemorating the 75th Anniversary of the Wellcome Trust

The Wellcome Trust seeks to achieve extraordinary improvements in human and animal health. It derives its vision, and the means to pursue it, from an extraordinary man. Sir Henry Wellcome led a fascinating life. He co-founded a company, Burroughs Wellcome & Co, which transformed the pharmaceutical industry in this country by blending innovative marketing techniques with a commitment to laboratory-based research and development. Nor were his ambitions limited to the overlapping spheres of science and industry. Wellcome's lifelong passion for the study of history resulted in the creation of a vast museum and library collection through which he hoped to tell the grand story of healing and disease in human society.

As both collector and entrepreneur, Wellcome recognised the potency of images: he even had a hand in the design of the unicorn symbol which adorned his company's products. It is fitting therefore that Sir Henry Wellcome: Backwood to Knighthood reveals Wellcome's story – his company, his collection and his bequest – through pictures as well as text.

It illustrates his remarkable journey from a rural upbringing on the plains of the United States to prosperous old age in England, and shows how the Wellcome Trust continues to follow his vision by funding ground-breaking biomedical research, and by placing such research in its cultural and historical contexts.

I am pleased to declare a special interest in the Wellcome story, not only as the current Chairman of the Trust, but also as someone whose own career begun with the Wellcome pharmaceutical company. I have the honour of being Chairman as we mark the Trust's 75th anniversary: as we take stock and consider his fascinating life, this lavishly illustrated work will act as a visual record of Sir Henry Wellcome's achievements and a reminder of the importance of his legacy.

Sir William Castell,
Chairman, The Wellcome Trust

Backwood to Knighthood

"Make no small plans for they have no power to stir the blood of man"
Daniel Hudson Burnham (1846–1912)

When Henry Wellcome was born in 1853 in Almond, Wisconsin, the territory of Alaska was still a part of the Russian Empire. The Dominion of Canada lay unfounded, the Suez and Panama canals did not exist and the dark continent of Africa was mostly unexplored by European man. Motor cars, manned flight, Polar exploration and the horrors of the first World War lay ahead in the future by at least half a century.

This year, 1853, also saw the beginning of the war in the Crimea where an Alliance of Britain, France and Turkey fought Russia. A war in which the number of men who died from illness, exposure and malnutrition was four times greater than the number who died as a result of enemy action. Young Henry's early life in the American North West was also affected by conflict, as the American Civil War began in 1861. Of more significance for the Wellcome family was the Sioux uprising of 1862, which would shatter their peaceful existence. This experience would remain with the thoughtful Henry Wellcome in the years to come.

Wellcome's life was to become a series of journeys, beginning with his apprenticeship in the developing American pharmaceutical industry. This would take him east to the cities of Chicago, Philadelphia, and eventually New York. Once qualified the young Henry Wellcome travelled extensively throughout North America as a commercial representative of McKesson and Robbins. In 1878 at the age of 25 he undertook an arduous expedition to South America, visiting Ecuador in particular, on behalf of this firm of druggists. His own detailed and descriptive account of this expedition reveals much about the character attributes of Henry Wellcome. It is also evident that the experience of these early travels would shape his future philosophy and life's work.

Wellcome's report to McKesson and Robbins, on the sustainability of harvesting Cinchona bark for the production of quinine, demonstrated that Wellcome was an extremely talented observer and reporter, with a keen eye for the finer details of the natural world of plants. His obvious concern for the welfare of the indigenous people (often engaged in the hazardous work of collecting and transporting the bark through inhospitable terrain) exposed his strong humanitarian instinct. Wellcome's comments on the meagre remuneration received by the Cinchona bark harvesters showed a sense of fairness and justice which became his bywords as a caring employer. The report's conclusion, that current methods of gathering the bark, would, before too long destroy the trees and render the species virtually extinct, gives us a glimpse of the forward thinking that sustained the success of Wellcome's own company. In this regard he would be ahead of his time. This expedition ignited the spark of Sir Henry's lifelong passion for medical research into tropical diseases. In particular, the quest for strategies to control malarial disease would become central to his life's work.

By the time Henry Wellcome boarded The City of Berlin in April 1880 for the transatlantic crossing to England, the strength of his character was already formed. In the years to come, initially in the Burroughs Wellcome partnership, and subsequently, as the sole owner of Wellcome and Co., this strength of character would be greatly tested. Furthermore, the tragic disintegration of his marriage to Syrie Wellcome nee Barnado would effect a deep personal loss from which he struggled to recover for many years.

An understanding of the diverse influence and impact of this prolific traveller, entrepreneur, philanthropist, collector and archaeology enthusiast is revealed to us in some measure by the pictorial archive left by Wellcome himself. Previous biographies, in particular Henry Wellcome by Robert Rhodes James, published in 1994, allow us to further grasp the complexities of a man whose vision of a better world would touch those who knew him personally, and many more worldwide who did not.

When Sir Henry Wellcome died in 1936 his contribution to the eradication of disease, and the prolonging of human life, was not yet apparent. Wellcome's enduring legacy is the successful continuation of the medical and scientific research that he had so passionately promoted throughout his remarkable life.

John A. Flannery

E.COURRET   LIMA.

Wellcome

1853	1861	1866	1872	1874	1876	1879	1880	1883	1884	1889
Birth of Henry Wellcome in Almond, Wisconsin USA.	Wellcome family trek to Garden City, Minn.	Henry leaves school and begins work in family drug store.	Moves east to study in Chicago	Graduation and move to New York City. Engaged by Caswell Hazard and Co., Druggists	Solomon Wellcome dies. Henry acquires post with McKesson Robbins	Henry invited by Silas Burroughs to take a European vacation	Burroughs Wellcome & Co. founded	The Snow Hill H.Q., London opens	Tabloid brand patented	Dartford factory opens
War begins in the Crimea	Outbreak of the American Civil War	Alfred Nobel invents dynam-ite	Home rule for Ireland	Disraeli becomes British prime minister	The first Boer War	Edison develops the electric light bulb	Laveran discovers the malaria parasite	The world's first sky-scraper built in Chicago	Krakatoa volcano erupts	French Panama Canal Company bankrupt
1853	1861	1866	1872	1874	1876	1879	1880	1883	1884	1889

World

Events

1895	1896	1901	1903	1909	1910	1917	1924	1931	1932	1936
Death of Silas Burroughs	H. W. Chairs the American Society, Thanksgiving Day Banquet London	Marriage to Syrie Barnardo	Henry Mounteney Wellcome is born	Report on the Panama Canal Project and separation from Syrie	Now a British Citizen and returns to Egypt and the Sudan	The Dartford works is expanded to support the production of World War I drugs and medical supplies	The Wellcome Foundation is established	Awarded Freedom of the Society of Apothecaries	Sir Henry is a Knight of the British Empire	Death of Sir Henry Wellcome

Marconi invents radio telegraphy	Start of the Klondike gold rush, U.S.A.	First Nobel prizes awarded	Henry Ford founds Ford Motor Company	Louis Blériot crosses the English Channel in an airplane	Marie Curie publishes Treatise on Radiography	Russian Revolution begins	Airship Z-R-3 crosses the Atlantic	Empire State Building completed	Over 30 million out of work worldwide	Edward VIII abdicates and becomes the Duke of Windsor He is succeeded by George VI.
1895	1896	1901	1903	1909	1910	1917	1924	1931	1932	1936

Events

Backwood...

"The boy who is going to make a great man must not make up his mind merely to overcome a thousand obstacles, but to win in spite of a thousand repulses and defeats."

Theodore Roosevelt

The Americans of the 1850s were motivated in much the same way as their modern counterparts. They were either pulled by the dream of a better life, or pushed by the fear of their diminishing circumstances. The Wellcome family of Freeman, Maine were no different in this respect. The struggle to subsist in the harsh winters of the north eastern Atlantic state had pushed 21 year old Solomon Wellcome into making the 1,000 mile journey to Wisconsin, a newly founded state on the western shore of Lake Michigan. Arriving in 1849, Solomon married Mary Curtis in 1850, and was soon joined in the bleak mid Wisconsin landscape by his parents Tim and Mary who would help him farm land south of Almond which was owned by his new wife. It was into this farming family that George Wellcome and his younger brother Henry were born in 1851 and 1853 respectively.

By 1861, which marked the start of the American Civil War, the Wellcome's were once again struggling to develop a life above subsistence level. Solomon's ill health and failures of the staple potato crop prompted a push westward once more. This second trek was also motivated by the uplifting reports of more bountiful prospects in the newly created frontier state of Minnesota. It was here that Solomon's elder brother Jacob had settled with his second wife, Sarah Houser, after the death of his first wife, Abigail Starbird, in 1856. Jacob was a physician and surgeon and had established a successful practice in Garden City.

With the Wisconsin farm sold, and their possessions loaded into a covered wagon, three generations of Wellcomes began the four week trek to Garden City, Blue Earth County, Minnesota. The ox - drawn wagon was just one of a group of 'prairie schooners' sailing in convoy for protection against potential hostile attack. In the event, the journey was completed safely, with the native tribes silently observing the incursion into their ancient hunting lands with emotions that would tragically soon transform into a burning resentment.

The diary kept by 14 year old Sallie Hester who trekked with her family from Missouri to California in 1849, graphically describes the experiences of the pioneering families. The diversity of the groups, the preparation of laying in stores, and the symbiotic relationship between the travellers and their stock of mules, oxen and horses. This method of travel required the wagon trails to follow the watercourses vital for the sustenance of all. The Wellcome's journey of 300 miles was small by comparison with that of the Hester family's 2,000 mile, five month odyssey to the Pacific coast, however, the adventurous spirit kindled around the camp fires had sparked a wanderlust in the young Henry Wellcome that would manifest itself in the not too distant future.

Upon reaching Garden City the Wellcome family settled quickly into the frontier community, the transition eased by Uncle Jacob's standing as physician and the owner of the drug store. Jacob was generous and caring towards his brother's family, providing employment and an opportunity to develop the store business.

Henry and his brother George attended the log cabin school alongside the other children of the settlers. It can be no coincidence that many of Wellcome's contemporaries, including his cousin Frank, were to pursue very ambitious careers in commerce, banking and real estate. Inhabiting a dangerous world where death from diphtheria was all too commonplace seemed to engender a steely resolve in the children of the frontier.

Et Pluribus Unum

Between the years 1850 and 1890, the Great Plains area, stretching from the Mississippi to the Rocky Mountains, would become populated by many nations as one. The plains had previously been a passage to be crossed with a trepidation equal to that of the Atlantic crossing. The collective stories of these diverse groups evolved into the epic legend that would eventually define the United States of America. Whilst the Europe that had been left behind would continue to struggle for influence and shares in the territory and markets of Africa and Asia, its exiles would strive to make their contributions to the New World. This settlement drive was a partnership between a government and its newest peoples, united in the belief of a 'manifest destiny'.

Above | The first money earned by Henry Wellcome

Right | Two illustrations of buffalo *

Opposite Page Top | Map of North American Indian localities

Opposite Page Bottom | North American Prairies *

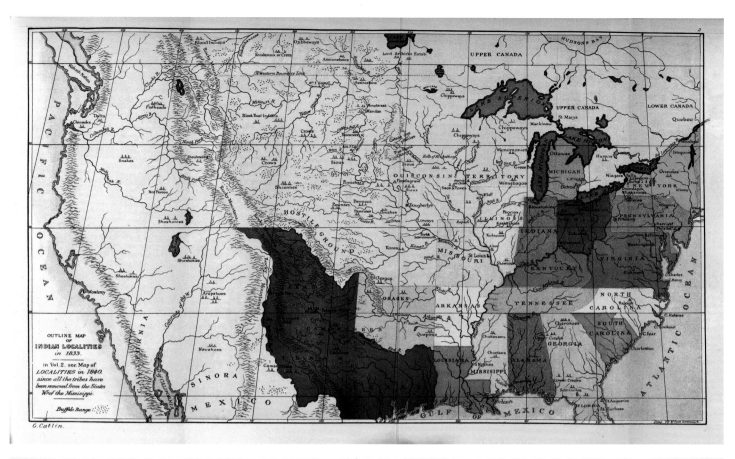

44

G. Catlin

Manifest Destiny

The varied people settling the Great Plains included the Wellcome family who derived from English, and previously, French stock. Their fellow settlers and neighbours in this vast landscape included Scandinavians and Germans. The populating of the Great Plains threw together people of varied skills and professions. Divisions naturally emerged between the likes of miners and prospectors, cattle ranchers and farmers. Life was hard, and tough times were endured by all vying for a stake in the future. When the civil war ended, former soldiers joined the ranks of those seeking a more peaceful life. Black men and women also headed north and west in search of greater opportunities and freedom from the prejudices they had endured in the southern states. The lifeline that eventually connected all of these people and their combined industry came with the completion of the transcontinental railroad in 1869. Chinese labourers were instrumental in the construction of this vital transport infrastructure. The connection to the railroad could make or break the fortunes of a fledgling community, and many promising settlements became ghost towns, quickly abandoned in favour of one more strategically placed. The railroad created the opportunity to ship increased numbers of cattle to market, improving profitability for the ranchers. Gold, silver and lead mines also gave rise to boom and bust communities in the frantic rush for prosperity. Fortunes made could also be quickly lost in the transition from one enterprise to another.

In the Great Plains, numerous tribes of Native Americans were overwhelmed as the agrarian machine, in time, turned the plains into the bread basket of the states, now united from "sea to shining sea". The nomadic hunters, whose traditional existence depended on the natural cycle of life were ultimately squeezed into pockets of land that were deemed surplus to the white man's requirements. Some, like the Winnebago, bravely attempted to adjust to the new way of life, alongside families like the Wellcomes. Others preferred to stand and fight for their way of life and were tragically decimated and defeated as a consequence.

Native America

"When I was a boy, the Sioux owned the world. The sun rose and set on their land..."

Sitting Bull

The Sioux word Minnesota, meaning cloudy water, accurately describes the river running through the state. Sadly, it might also have described the muddled political situation facing the new settlers. The idyllic landscape into which the Wellcome family had migrated in 1861 was indeed as bountiful as Dr. J. W. B. Wellcome had described in the letters written to his brother, Solomon. The 'backwoods' surrounding the small towns provided the raw material for building and the soil was fertile for farming. This 'land of plenty' was, of course, home not just to the settlers, but traditionally to the native Sioux, Winnebago and other tribes. Whilst the Winnebago were mostly welcoming and friendly, resentment had been growing in the Sioux chief, Little Crow, for some time.

The settlement and agriculturisation of the land west of the Mississippi was subject to deals negotiated by agents on behalf of the U.S. Government. Unfortunately, the deals were often undermined by individual traders to the point where remuneration for land was not commensurate with the value. The tense situation was exacerbated when settlers, anxious to stake their individual claims to a new life in the West, moved in to the region before the due process of the U.S. government was completed and payment concluded. In 1862 the U.S. government was preoccupied with a bitter civil war with 11 mainly southern states which had ceded from the Union over the issue of slave emancipation. All over North America the diverse values and beliefs of indigenous and new populations were stretching tolerance and understanding to breaking point.

On the 17th August 1862, the Sioux of the southern Minnesota river valley launched a swift, rampaging attack on the far flung settler homesteads. The lives of the Wellcome family were very soon in danger as New Ulm was attacked, and the safety of Garden City was threatened by Little Crow and the Sioux. The outlying farms were surprised by the speed and ferocity of the attack and many settlers were brutally murdered in the initial onslaught. With military manpower in short supply, the settlers, including the Wellcome family, resourcefully organised resistance to repel the attacks on the outposts. Jacob Wellcome enhanced his status by tirelessly treating the wounded with the able assistance of young Henry. Eventually, reinforcements arrived and by the end of the month, General Pope had relieved the situation and dispersed Little Crow and his braves. Little Crow was subsequently caught and killed by the pursuing U.S. forces and hundreds of his followers were captured, imprisoned and tried by the military at Fort Snelling. In the aftermath, the growing settler population, fuelled by horrific reports of the deaths on the farmlands, clamoured for revenge. Thirty-eight prisoners, whose death sentences were not commuted by President Lincoln, were publicly hanged at Mankato on the 26th December 1862. The remainder were banished to the Dakota territories. The Minnesota settlements were then reinforced by Pope's troops.

This tragic episode had dire consequences for the native population who had not supported Little Crow's guerrilla tactics. Increasing numbers of Sioux and other tribes caught in the "crossfire" were forcibly relocated to lands devoid of the basic requirements for sustaining their traditional way of life. Although many of his near neighbours had suffered tragic fates in the Sioux uprising, Henry Wellcome would retain a lifelong empathy and solid respect for the native American peoples and their ancient traditions and culture.

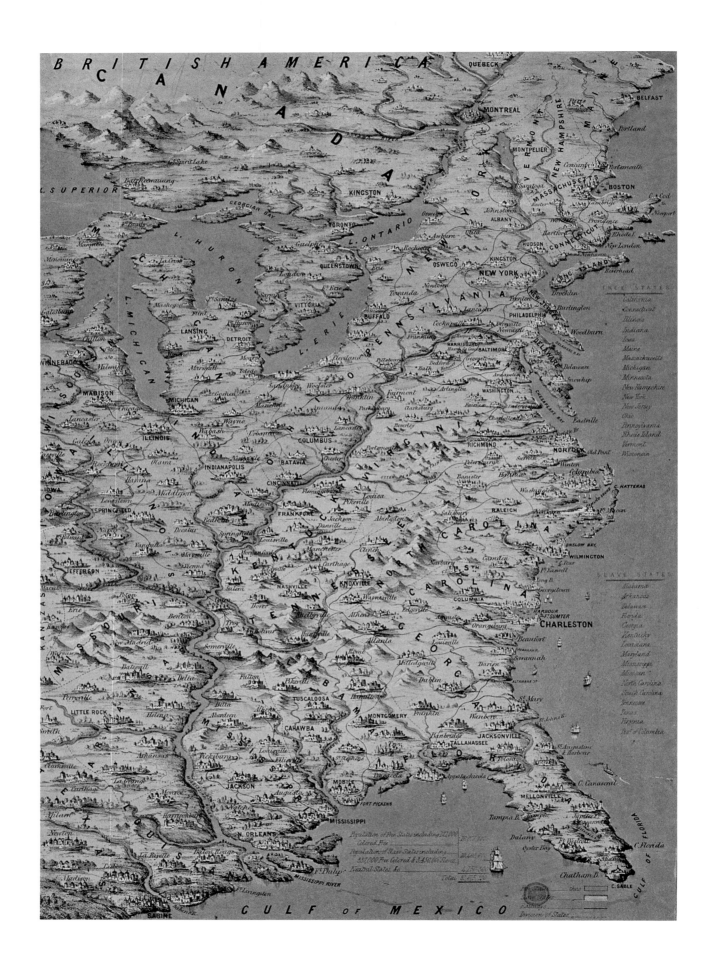

North American Indians

Before the arrival of the white man, the North American Indians lived a life entirely dependent upon the forces of nature that enveloped them. Their perspective of the world was shaped by a healthy respect for the climactic conditions and the animals and plants that had sustained them for centuries. The plains Indians, approximately thirty tribes, coexisted with buffalo, bear, wolves, eagles, antelope and deer. Life on the plains was only sustainable in groups working together. The transient lifestyle was also a response to the migration of the vast herds of bison, later known as buffalo. These animals were utilised in numerous ways, not least for food, clothing and shelter. Up to a dozen hides would fashion a teepee. The rapid American expansion into the West reduced the herds almost to extinction by the end of the 1870s. The North American Indians could not conceive of land ownership, and were unable to adjust to the introduction of this European ideal. It is also thought that more of the native population died as a result of foreign diseases than fighting the invasion of their homeland.

Indian Uprising

Siaux Massacre One of Worst Incidents in History of U. S.

Eight Minnesota Counties Were Devastated Aug. 18-20, 1862—Two Thousand Settlers and Soldiers Were Killed

The anniversary of the Custer massacre and the participation of the remnant of the once powerful Sioux nation in the events marking that date brings to the mind of the people of Minnesota, especially the valley of the Minnesota river, the horror of 64 years ago: just 14 years previous to the destruction of Custer's band by the Sioux warriors under Sitting Bull.

It was one of those awful incidents of the early development of our country with which history is so replete. Without question the three days following Aug. 17 1862, were the most terrible history has ever related: the worst massacre of Indian history. During these three days a population of 30,000 occupying 18 counties of Minnesota, were scattered all over the middle west—into Mississippi, Wisconsin, Illinois, Indiana, Ohio, and some to their former homes in New England; eight counties of the territory were completely devasted; many hamlets, villages and towns destroyed, and more than 2000 white settlers and soldiers killed, besides several hundred taken captives to suffer untold horrors at the hands of their fiendish captors, and a property loss estimated at $2,500,000.

IN TWO DISTRICTS

The Sioux Indians of Minnesota were divided into two great districts by the federal agents with whom they had been treating relative to relinquishment of lands for white settlement. The northern natives were termed the Upper Sioux and the lower, or southern, the Lower Sioux. Little Crow was the chief, arbitrary and cunning, of the Lower tribes. He was able and, above all, a fighter. It is estimated that his warriors numbered more than 6000 before the outbreak in 1862. There were sub-chiefs, but they were under the sway of the eloquent and powerful Little Crow.

Briefly, the causes of the massacre, which began on Aug. 18, 1862, were these: Settlers had found the wonderful richness of the valley of the Minnesota and flocked there in thousands. It became necessary for the government to treat with the Sioux for the land of these settlers, and an agreement was reached under which the Indian chief was to receive a stated amount and an annual payment. These settlements were always satisfactory to the Indians as long as the money lasted, but, as soon as it was spent, dissatisfaction arose. Unfortunately, instead of paying the money to the chief as agreed for distribution to the Indians, it was paid to a trader; the Indians claiming they were cheated.

Trouble had been brewing for several years over the advancement of settlers and enroachments on both sides. The Sioux were not only powerful, but warlike. Little Crow was wise enougr to see that, in 1862, the nation was divided in the civil war, and if he ever was to strike a blow against the hated whites, then was the time.

LITTLE CROW CALLED FINAL COUNCIL OF SUB-CHIEFS

and, during the night, the women and children were conducted to St. Peter. The defenders of the town were, finally, forced to retreat, but not until a part of the buildings had been destroyed by fire; the remainder suffered at the hands of the victorious Sioux.

During this time, the commanders of the forts throughout the valley were sending hurried messages to St. Paul and other fortified towns to the east, as well as the south, for reinforcements. The scattered forces of the government, 30 in one fort, 40 in another, and similar numbers in others, were finally assembled at Fort Ridgley. The combined force numbered about 15 soldiers, but they had been augmented by hundreds of settlers—men who were willing to defend their homes at any cost.

On the following day, Little Crow decided he was strong enough to take Fort Ridgley and made an assault with all the fire and desperation of his nature. His men advanced to within a rifle shot of the fort and, at a given signal, with wild war-whoops, they rushed upon the fort. They expected resistance, but it was more severe than Little Crow had suspected. Many ruses were tried to lead the soldiers out of the fort and into ambush. One was a favorite of the crafty natives.

KNEW FORT WOULD EXPECT REINFORCEMENTS

They knew the people in the fort would expect reinforcements. A year before the massacre they had insisted that the government should supply them with civilian clothes; as they desired to dress as the white man. The clothing was supplied, little realizing to what use it would be put. The defenders of the fort eagerly looked for relief. At some distance from the fort and coming apparently from the rear of the enemy, a troup of about 60 men were seen advancing. They were dressed as white people; they were well armed, every man with a gun and ammunition. The whites thought it was the expected reinforcement.

Between the fort and the coming men was a small, but determined band of Indians. The white soldiers thought to clear a path for their relievers, and left the fort in a mad dash, only to walk into an ambush. The supposed relief was composed of Indian warriors dressed as whites to deceive the soldiers and lead them into the planned ambush.

Fort Ridgley held out, however, and much damage was done the Siouxs. How many natives were killed was never known, for the Indians always carried their dead and wounded from the battlefield and secreted them so the whites could never tell what destruction they had wrought. The defense of the fort, however, with the stubborn defense of New Ulm, broke the strength of the warriors under Little Crow, and the following day they began a retreat up the valley. It is without question that the stubborn resistance of the white soldiers, aided by hundreds of settlers, some of them armed only with knives, saved hundreds of people from massacre.

Many of the refugees, who rushed to

Left | Press cutting from Henry Wellcome's personal papers, 'Indian Rising 1862'

Below | * Information on the back of the photograph reads: 'Son of A. J. Jewett, who's Father, Mother, Grandfather and Grandmother were massacred at Garden City, Minnesota. This boy was taken by the heels and his head beaten against a log and left for dead. He was found unconscious by my uncle, Dr. J. W. B. W., who assisted in doctoring his wounds.' 1865

Opposite Top | Indian attack on New Ulm, Minnesota, August 1862

Opposite Bottom | * Information on the back of the photograph reads: 'Andrew Jewett's farm, where his Father and Mother, Himself and Wife and Tyler were massacred by the Indians at the Garden City. A. J. Jewett was born in Boston and studied law with Lawyer Wells, formerly governor of Maine.'

*Editors note: the Jewett's Farm deaths occurred in 1865

neighboring tribes, but ... no evidence that they actually took part in the massacre. The chiefs, after a ... discussion, decided to ... ... sota valley of all white settlers—30,-000 in all. They realized that the troops stationed at Fort Ridgley and other fortifications in the district, as well as the number of white troops at the Lower Agency were insufficient to protect the settlers. These fortifications had been drained for the civil war. It was also decided to strike at as many places as possible at the same time.

Just where the first blow was struck is not known; for there were so many outbreaks during the early hours of the morning of Aug. 18, 1862, and so few saved. It came like a bolt of lightning, striking at a score of places at one time. At the Lower Agency, a trading post and headquarters of the government agent in control of the Indians who had accepted aid in establishing themselves on farms, were about 200 people—men, women and children. New Ulm boasted a population of nearly a thousand. St. Peter also was a town of more than a thousand people. And, all through the valley were smaller towns, as well as hundreds of farms on both sides of the river.

Early on the morning of Aug. 18, Little Crow and many of his warriors mingled with the whites at the Lower Sioux agency. His men, fully armed, placed themselves at strategic points about the agency; some in the store, some in the headquarters, some in all the buildings to which they would be admitted, and others about the houses. All acted as though they were on an accustomed holiday. At the given signal, which was the killing of the agent by Little Crow, every native in the agency began the attack. Men were shot or tomahawked, women and children were murdered in their homes, or where they had rushed for safety at the first realization of the outbreak. Within 30 minutes the Lower Agency was a scene of slaughter; its entire population was either killed, captive or in flight, only to be pursued by the blood-frenzied savages.

The story of the Lower agency is the same story that was told at Nicollet, New Ulm and nearly a score of other settlements and towns. At the same time, small bands of Indians, by pre-arrangement, went to farms, to the scattered mills / and little villages, spreading death, fire and destruction at every hand. By 10 o'clock that morning the entire valley was aroused by the horrible spectacle of burning towns and villages. Even those, who were not among the first attacked, realized what the distant clouds of smoke meant, and all hastily resorted to flight, some little noting in which direction they went.

WORKED RAPIDLY

The work of the Indians was rapid. One town or village ravaged, it was fired and the warriors hurried to the next, destroying everything as they went. Death and flames marked the path; the path of the divided forces of Little Crow. All during the day of Aug. 18 and far into the night the savage scourge filled the valley with horror. Scarcely had they rested for a few hours during the night before the work of another day began: the work of clearing the valley of all whites—a work of massacre and death.

Flushed with their easy victories in capturing the smaller towns, the Indians next turned their attention to the larger ones, and even the forts and defenses. Little Ulm, which had a few hours' notice of the coming disaster, feebly attempted to defend itself. This defense checked the onrush of the savages to the smaller villages beyond, and gave the people an opportunity to seek safety. The defense of Little Ulm was stubborn, though the inhabitants fought with, no hope of defeating the tremendous hordes with whom they were confronted. Time was given, however, for a plan of escape to the forts,

Boston Herald July 4, 1926

Aug. 19. It harbored more than 9000. This rush of poor frightened people, who ... their homes without saving a thing; all without food, sufficient clothing, and many of them wounded, offered a problem to the people of St. Peter, but the residents of the town took up the task of feeding, clothing and attending the sufferers manfully.

OFFERED NO SECURITY

St. Peter, while a haven, did not offer much security. Had Fort Ridgley fallen before the Indian hoards, or had Little Crow proved his strategy by refusing to attack the fort, but gone to St. Peter instead, the story of the Minnesota valley massacre would have read still more horrible. The town was almost defenseless; it was crowded with 9000 women, children and wounded; practically all the fighting strength had joined the force that was opposing the Sioux. Its destruction would have been complete, and the number of dead in that town alone would have been more than in all the valley.

Little Crow was apparently flushed with his easy victories and wanted to destroy the fighting force of the whites before the reinforcements he knew eventually would come, arrived. Following the defeat at Fort Ridgley, Little Crow turned his army to the north, destroying as he went. He swept a path 200 miles long and 50 miles wide; that path was filled with death and desolation. Where 30,000 people had dwelt in peace and plenty a week before, now there was not a live whiteman, woman or child; where there had been thousands of homes, not one remained in its entirety; where scores of towns and villages flourished with the promise of greater wealth and prosperity, not one remained. The counties of Brown, Renville, Murray, Jackson, Martin, Watonwan, Cottonwood, Monongalia, Kandiyohi and Lincoln were wiped off the map as far as the white man was concerned, and the inhabitance of 10 adjoining counties had fled for their lives; believing that the red scourge would fall upon them.

Government reinforcements were rushed to the valley and placed on the trail of the retreating Siouxs until far into September.

They came from every direction where the government could spare troops. The retreat of the Indians and pursuit of the white soldiers was only another story of such experiences. As soon as the fortunes of war turned against Little Crow, his sub-chiefs deserted him and made peace with the commanders of their pursuers as best they could.

His whole band was finally broken up and scattered to whatever safe refuge they could find. Many of them were overtaken, identified by natives who had surrendered and ready to do anything to save their own lives, and hundreds killed or taken prisoners.

DESERTED BY FOLLOWING

Little Crow, at least, was deserted by his entire following. With his son, a boy of 16 years, he sought safety in the south, but was overtaken on July 3, 1863, recognized and killed; his son was taken prisoner. Others of his scattered band were captured to the number of 303. Of this number, 39 were finally hung at Mankato on Dec. 26, 1862, and the remainder released.

The only bright feature gleaned from the whole story was the faithfulness of some Indian chieftains like Standing Buffalo, John Other Day, who rescued 62 from the massacre at Yellow Medicine, and a few others who refused to aid their brethren in the destruction of their white friends.

The power of the Lower Sioux was broken for a while, the government placed larger forces of men in the defenses, and settlers again populated the rich valley, but the terrible days following the Sioux council of Aug. 17, 1862, will never be forgotten in Minnesota. It was the most horrible of all the Indian massacres on this continent.

Left | 'Indian Rising 1862': Press cutting from Boston Herald July 11th, 1926

Below Top | Description of E. P. Evans' Hotel, Garden City, Minnesota and how it was used each night by the women and children to shelter during the Great Sioux War.

Below Bottom | Photograph of E. P. Evans' Hotel

Opposite Page | Portrait of Dr. J. W. B. Wellcome

When surrounded by Indians during the great Sioux war this building was then being built, frame-up & rough boards only & women & children we gathered here each night - The town was guarded by a series of circles of pickets & a special reserve force ... with their weapons camped about this building -

The Pocahontas Portrait

In the early seventeenth century the Virginia Company of London camped on a swampy, mosquito infested site on the James River, (the settlement would become Jamestown, Virginia). By 1608 the depleted group of would-be adventurers and traders had become dependent on the Powhatan Indians to supplement their food and water supplies. The indigenous tribes worked together in an alliance known as the Powhatan Confederacy. Consequently, at this stage, they held the upper hand in the political power struggle with the English, as the settlers came to rely upon the native-grown corn crop.

Pocahontas came to the attention of the English in 1607, by dramatically pleading for the life of Captain John Smith who was to be executed by the decree of her father, Powhatan. The "Indian Princess" then became a pawn in the 'waiting game' played by the English while they reinforced their numbers in the region. In 1613 Pocahontas was kidnapped and held to ransom by Captain Samuel Argall. While in captivity she became married to Englishman John Rolfe and gave birth to a son named Thomas. In 1617 Pocahontas was taken to England and presented at court as American royalty to generate financial investment for the "New World" venture.

MARRIAGE OF POCAHONTAS.

Reports suggest that as a result of his daughter's kidnapping Powhatan became indecisive in his bargaining, ceding power to others, including his brother Opechancanough. It is now thought by some scholars that the kidnapping and subsequent "political marriage" was a deliberate ploy by the English to compromise and weaken the power of the Powhatan Confederacy. Opinion remains divided as to what degree Pocahontas was rebellious in nature, and complicit in the English scheming. Sadly, she paid for the adventure with her life, as she died, aged 23 years, during the visit to England in 1617 and was buried in Gravesend.

Henry Wellcome exhibited his copy of the 1616 Simon de Passe portrait at the Chicago World's Fair in 1893. His subsequent gesture of presenting it to the American Congress became the subject of protracted negotiations and scrutiny. Van de Passe's portrait is still the subject of controversy as critics now believe Pocahontas was inaccurately portrayed with European features. Watercolour paintings by English artist John White c.1585 portray the very different tattooed features of Powhatan Algonquin women.

Other Wellcome Collection portraits from:

Rinehart, F. A. (1899) Rinehart's Indians.

Omaha: F. A. Rinehart

Above | Naiche, hereditary chief of the Chirucahua

Above | Bartelda - San Carlos Apache | Native America

Dr. William Duncan and the Tsimshian tribe

In 1887 Henry Wellcome was moved to write a book entitled The Story of Metlakahtla. The real life hero of this story was William Duncan, born in 1832 in Bishop Burton, in the East Riding of Yorkshire, England. Duncan's remarkable story began with a journey around Cape Horn in 1856. When Duncan landed in the Pacific North West he encountered the native Indian Tsimshian tribes and considered them to be of a savage nature. British Columbia, or B.C. was Before Christ as far as Duncan was concerned. Subsequently the "civilising" of the natives became his life's mission. With Wellcome's support, Duncan established a utopian Christian community aimed at "saving" the heathen populace through industry and the worship of a Christian God. In this respect, Duncan was not dissimilar to his fellow Yorkshireman, Titus Salt (see A Time for Work, a Time for Play). Duncan tackled the savagery head on, as two rams might, when meeting on a narrow Pennine pass. He may well have regaled the Tsimshian chief Lecaic with the Yorkshire anecdote concerning the three known types of men. "There are Yorkshiremen, there are those who wish they were Yorkshiremen, and there are those with no ambition at all". Wellcome's empathy with the disadvantaged natives of North America and Canada, manifested itself in the financial support for William Duncan's work. This well meaning support, for what can only be described as Christian Paternalism, punctuates the work of the late Victorian era's philanthropists. Wellcomes work in the Sudan was initially targeted towards the eradication of disease in Khartoum. Inevitably, the Christian ethos soon spilled over into the archaeological excavations at Jebel Moya. The temperance and work ethic imposed on the populations of both tundra and desert were characteristics of the imperialistic age. However, looking back through the mists of harsh Alaskan winters, William Duncan and Henry Wellcome's actions may well have ensured that the Tsimshian tribes endured a safe transition into the 20th century when many others did not fare so well.

THE STORY OF METLAKAHTLA.

CHAPTER I.

DAYS OF PERIL.

A CIVILIZING work without parallel, alike remarkable for the original thought and genius displayed, and for the heroic courage in execution; is that conceived and carried out by William Duncan, in British Columbia, on the North Pacific coast, near Alaska.

Captain (now Admiral) Prevost, returning to England from a cruise in the North Pacific, excited great public interest by his account of the terrible state of barbarism that prevailed there. Mr. Duncan, sacrificed a highly lucrative position in a business house and started out for this field under the auspices of the Church Missionary Society, taking passage in a Hudson's Bay Company's sailing vessel, which rounded Cape Horn. On reaching Vancouver Island, Sir James Douglas, then the governor of the Hudson's Bay Company, urged in the strong-

NATIVE HOUSE WITH CARVED TOTEM POLE.

American Apprentice

"The principal goal of education is to create men who are capable of doing new things, not simply repeating what other generations have done."

Jean Piaget

WELLCOME'S MAGIC INK.
The Greatest Wonder of the Age !
This is something entirely New and Novel !
Directions.
Write with quill or golden pen. on white paper. No trace is visible until held to the fire, when it becomes very black.

PREPARED ONLY BY
H. S. wellcome,
GARDEN CITY,   MINN.

School was initially completed for Henry Wellcome by the age of thirteen. Young Henry's development from practical joker and inventor of Wellcome's Magic Ink to becoming a serious student of pharmacy took place gradually. This transition may well have been a case of nurture rather than nature, as the only immediate opportunity open to the young school leaver was to work in the family drug store.

In terms of influence, it would seem that Wellcome's Uncle, Jacob, who had established the drug store and built up his medical practice around it, would be the ideal role model for any young man with an inquisitive mind. The reputation of Dr. Wellcome was now the stuff of legends following his heroic, selfless acts in treating the wounded settlers during the Sioux uprising. Young Henry had seen a great deal of this work at first hand.

Wellcome also came to know H. J. Barton, a chemist from Leeds, England who had also established a small pharmaceutical practice in Garden City. Dr. William Worrall Mayo from Manchester, England had also found himself practicing medicine in Le Sueur, Minnesota and was a colleague of Dr. Wellcome. Mayo had also performed heroically when the Sioux had attacked New Ulm. The Yorkshireman, Barton and the Lancastrian, Mayo would apply the first tugs on a thread that would eventually draw Henry Wellcome to

England. When the Mayo family moved from Le Sueur to Rochester, Dr. Mayo recommended Henry Wellcome to Poole and Geisinger, a pharmaceutical chemist with a dispensary below Mayo's office. It was here that Wellcome began work as a prescription clerk in 1870. With this position, Wellcome took on the lifelong role of supporting his family financially. The fortunes of his immediate family, left behind in Garden City, were constrained by the preaching vocations and ill health of Henry's father, Solomon Wellcome. Henry's older brother, George, would subsequently follow in his father's ecclesiastical footsteps.

While Henry was happy and contented with his position in Rochester, nurtured by the kindness of the Mayo family, he was also actively encouraged by Dr. Mayo to gain academic qualifications in his chosen field. Again, with Dr. Mayo's help, he made the move further east in May 1872 to study at the Chicago College of Pharmacy. At the time, Wellcome's father, Solomon, was unsure about this ambitious move, perhaps forgetting his own life changing odyssey twenty-two years previously. In order to obtain lodgings in the recently fire ravaged city, and pay the college fees for the three evenings per week tuition, Wellcome had taken a position with Dr. Thomas Whitfield. However, Dr. Whitfield's excessive demands on Henry Wellcome's time prompted him to find better prospects for employment and education with a further move eastward.

In July 1873 Wellcome gained employment with Mr. Heisher (apothecary) in Philadelphia. It was here that he would join his new friend from Chicago, Frederick Power. A great camaraderie ensued, sustaining both men through to graduation at the Philadelphia College of Pharmacy.

Phila. March 4ᵗʰ 1874

Dear Folks at Home
I have graduated and
am happy
yes — I am Happy
So rejoice with me and
be exceeding glad
With much affection

New York City 1st May 1874

Wellcome's graduation was a source of great joy and happiness to him. In a note sent to the folks at home he urged them to rejoice and be glad. With this victory now won, Wellcome did not waste time in capitalising on his success. On the 1st May 1874, Henry Wellcome moved to New York to take up employment with Caswell Hazard & Co., Druggists. In August of the same year, Wellcome celebrated his 21st birthday. A letter home at the time reveals his single minded determination to make the most of his opportunities amidst the recurring discussion with his parents on ambition, wealth and morality. As Henry Wellcome's prospects increase proportionally to his endeavours, it becomes apparent in the correspondence that his attitude hardens with regard to trusting in God alone to provide. His straitened circumstances as a struggling student in the cities of Chicago and Philadelphia revealing to him that in future the best way to help the poor was by not being one them.

To this end Wellcome dedicated himself to learning the details of the national and international drug trade in which Caswell Hazard were engaged. Two years later in May 1876 Solomon Wellcome died before his fiftieth year, leaving Henry Wellcome as the sole breadwinner for the family from which he was exiled. That same month, Wellcome secured a well paid post as a travelling sales representative for the New York firm of McKesson and Robbins. Wellcome was soon into his stride, securing large orders from doctors and pharmacists for the high quality gelatine coated pills that McKesson and Robbins manufactured.

The travelling salesmen navigated from city to city using the expanding railway network through the hub of Chicago. The distribution of orders would follow the sales via the same network. Wellcome travelled extensively within the United States throughout this period. His success as a representative, and growing reputation within the American pharmaceutical industry would lead to McKesson Robbins now setting Wellcome his greatest challenge to date. In 1878, Wellcome was dispatched to South America on a field research expedition.

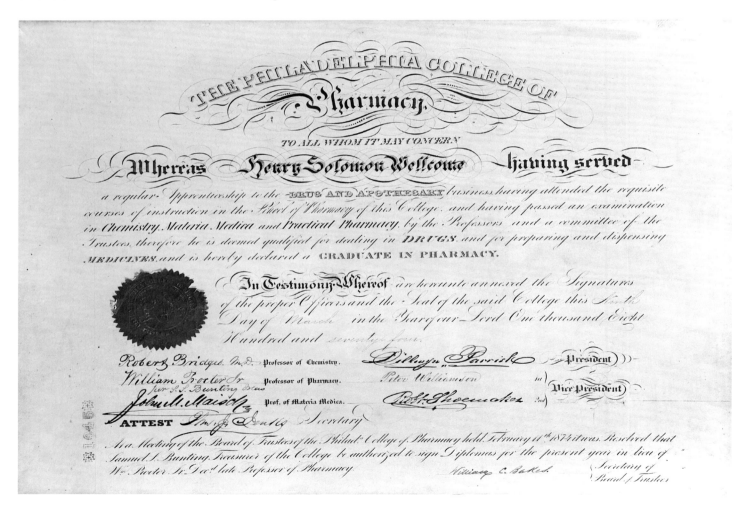

4

happiness though often humilliated
even ~~in~~ the dust to their persecutors,
Now you used to quote that
passage which says "He that hasteth
to be rich is not wise." And I
know I used to think a great deal
about when I should be able to
lay up wealth, I have lived out
my life thus far by impulses
many may have looked upon my move
as hasty, I have made up my mind
for each move with a sudden impulse
though I have usualy considered these
well before putting them into execution
now I have always had a desire for
WEALTH and still have but I
do believe that passage of scripture is
true and another which should
be complied with it is "Him that

132 Thames St.
Newport, R.I.

ESTABLISHED 1780.

Cor. 5th Ave. & 24th St. N.Y.
Cor. 6th Ave. & 39th St. N.Y.

CASWELL, HAZARD & CO.
DRUGGISTS.

New York _____ 187.

strives not for earthly blessings
is not wise, too many want
God to raise their crops trust & guid,
the grain and almost put into their
bellies, I do believe that God helps
those who help themselves & I believe
that "He often chastneth those he loveth"
Now I want to attain wealth
but I want to live a life devoted
to the true God and to mankind,
my purpose is strong but my mind
is WEAK. You know my plans
for future I think, I intend to remain in N.Y.
2 or 3 years longer and then return
to the WEST, probably "Chicago"
my stay in N. York is not for the
purpose of making money but for
cultivating my knowledge of business
as can only be learned by practical

The Cinchona Expedition of 1878

Henry Wellcome's report into the diminishing Cinchona forests of South America greatly enhanced his growing reputation in the medical world. Cinchona bark was the source for the production of quinine which was extremely efficacious as a daily regimen in malaria blighted regions.

This highly dangerous trek through the remote regions of Ecuador and Peru would bring Wellcome to the attention of ambitious men beyond the offices of McKesson and Robbins. At the same time as Wellcome was traversing South America, "On the hurricane deck of a mule", another Philadelphia graduate, Silas Burroughs, was engaged in a fact finding mission to Europe. It would not be too long before their meandering paths would converge.

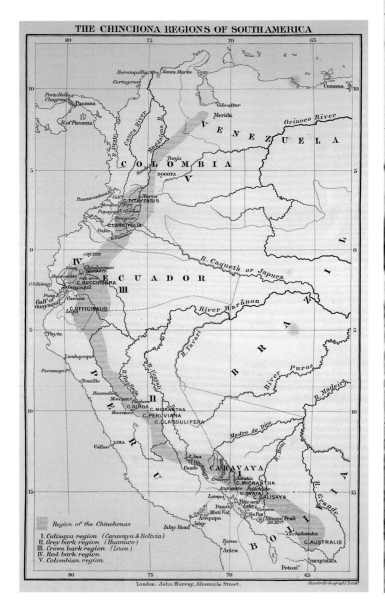

hurricane deck of a mule

J. Baiz

through Central and South America

CINCHONA OFFICINALIS, *Linn.*

D.Blair F.L.S. ad sicc. del. et lith.

Hanhart imp.

Above | A Quinine plant. From: Bentley, R. and Trimen, H. (1880) Medicinal Plants.

Transatlantic Business

"It is a better and a wiser thing to be a starved apothecary than a starved poet; so back to the shop Mr. John, back to plasters, pills and ointment boxes."

John Gibson Lockhart

In 1878, Silas Mainville Burroughs founded S. M. Burroughs and Co.. He had graduated from the Philadelphia College of Pharmacy in 1877, where he had specialised in the manufacture of compressed tablets. This innovation in the production of measured medicines was the single spark that ignited Burroughs ambition to build a worldwide business. Working as a travelling representative of Wyeth and Co., Burroughs had constructed an impressive network of contacts in the fast growing pharmaceutical industry. With a roving eye on the European market, John Wyeth had agreed to the founding of Burrough's new company in London. This company evolved into an agency for Wyeth's products which was the seed from which the Burroughs Wellcome international business would grow, and eventually flourish.

Silas Burroughs had the vision to see the vast potential market outside the United States for the new compressed medicines. He also had the confidence in his abilities as a salesman to expand the business beyond the shores of Great Britain, into mainland Europe and beyond. However, he also recognised that in order to do this he would need an able partner to hold the London based business together.

Across the Atlantic, Henry Wellcome, aged twenty-six, was also engaged in a foreign enterprise. Wellcome was undertaking the survey and report on the Ecuadorian Cinchona forests as the source of raw material for the production of quinine. The report was produced for his employers, McKesson Robbins of New York City.

By January 1879, Burroughs was writing to his fellow Philadelphia College graduate with the idea of Wellcome taking a vacation in Europe. The letter suggested that the vacation might also serve as a fact finding business trip.

By August of the same year, Burroughs correspondence was more detailed in proposing a partnership. By October, Burroughs had suggested that if Wellcome could secure an agency agreement with McKesson Robbins, this would enable a balanced partnership, complimenting Burrough's own agency agreement with John Wyeth. A further five months would elapse before Wellcome eventually crossed the Atlantic in early April 1880. The time had not been wasted, as Wellcome had successfully negotiated a five year agreement with McKesson Robbins to market their products in all territories outside of the United States. Wellcome had managed his exit strategy superbly, remaining on good terms with his former employers, with the new symbiotic agency agreement binding them together for the business expansion. The agency agreement would be a vital bargaining tool in securing an equitable partnership with Burroughs who was already established, however tenuously, in London. As both men would discover before too long, an enduring partnership can be difficult to sustain when one or other of the partners has an inherent belief in their initial contribution or seniority. Wellcome had cautiously kept the news of his agency agreement to himself, choosing to keep his 'powder dry' until he had seen the partnership prospects for himself. On board The City of Berlin, embarking on the less travelled west to east crossing, Henry Wellcome wrote to his mother. In this letter he reported his determined mood and full commitment to making a success of the venture. Awkwardly, he is also compelled to explain his decision to ignore the advice of his Uncle Isaac, who had advised against investing a lifetime in a continent where self interest made war inevitable. Nevertheless, a safe crossing ensued.

"God Helps Those Who Help Themselves"

Arriving in London for an initial meeting with Silas Burroughs, Henry Wellcome was surprised to learn that the proposed partnership plan had not been cleared with John Wyeth. Prudently, Wellcome insisted that Burroughs travelled immediately to Philadelphia to address the issue, whilst he would travel to Europe to settle his own unfinished business. Wellcome was anxious to meet with his dear friend Frederick Belding Power in Strasbourg.

Wellcome and Power had previously discussed the possibilities of combining their talents in a commercial enterprise. Wellcome was now naturally concerned that Power should hear the news of his new partnership plan at first hand. Wellcome characteristically managed to throw a positive light on the situation, assuring his friend that his academic attributes would be greatly valued, should he wish to join the new organisation when the time was right. This effort to nurture and preserve a sound friendship would prove to be of mutual benefit, as Power would become vital to the future success of Burroughs Wellcome & Co. Ltd.

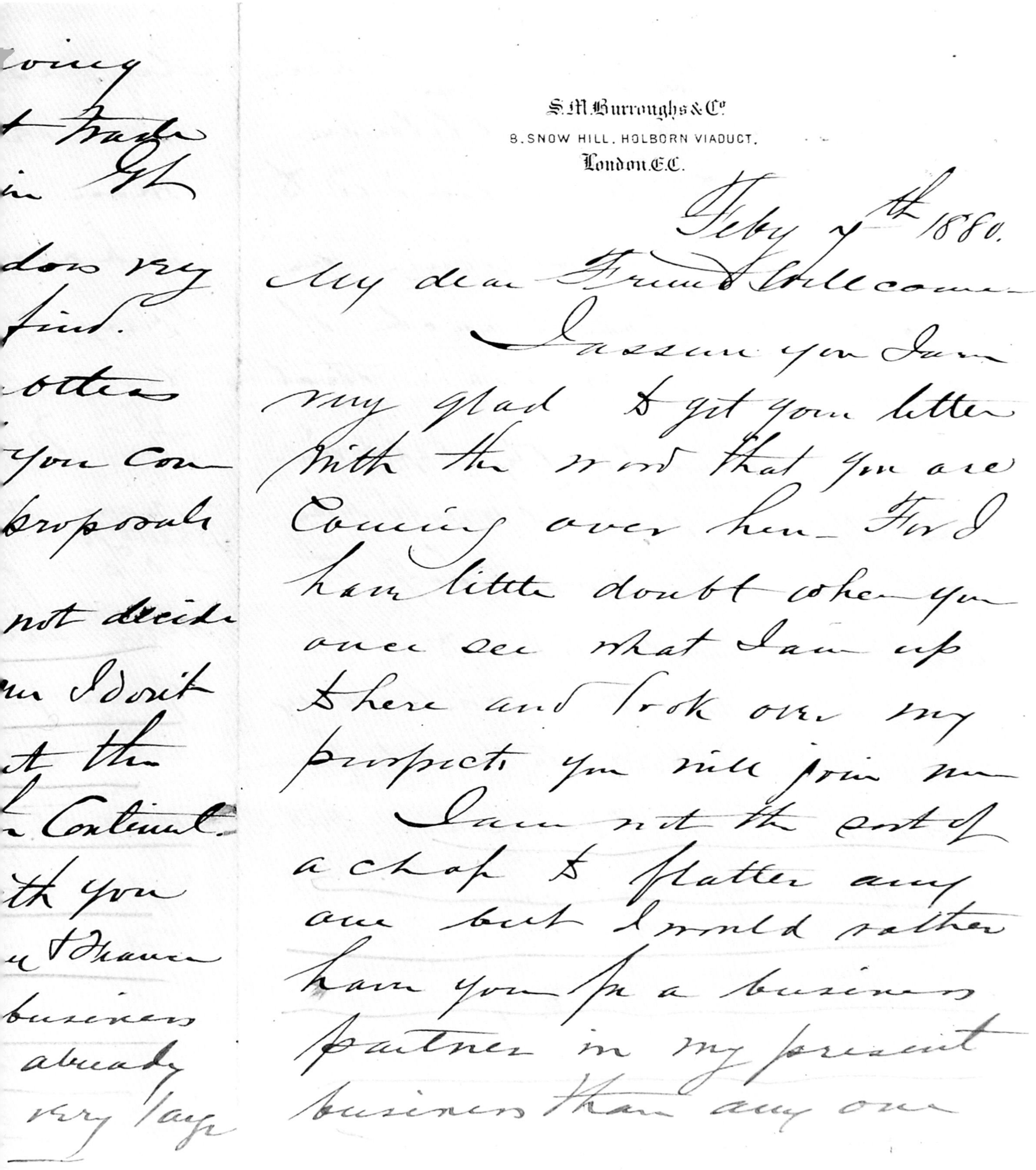

S.M.Burroughs&Cº
8.SNOW HILL. HOLBORN VIADUCT.
London.E.C.

Feby 7th 1880.

My dear Friend Wellcome

I assure you I am very glad to get your letter with the word that you are Coming over here — For I have little doubt when you once see what I am up there and look over my prospects you will join me

I am not the sort of a chap to flatter any one but I would rather have you for a business partner in my present business than any one

(left margin, partial)
...roing ...t trade ...in Sh ...does very ...find. ...ottos ...you can ...proposals ...not decide ...n I don't ...t the ...Continent. ...th you ...u I have ...business ...already ...very large

Burroughs Wellcome & Co. Deed of Partnership
27th September 1880

The partnership agreement was for a 10 year period with an option for either partner to terminate after five years (subject to 6 months written notice). Of the £2,000 initial capital investment, Burroughs invested £1,200 and Wellcome £800 after borrowing £550 from his partner at 10% interest per annum. Profits and losses were to be directly proportionate to investment, however at any time after two years Wellcome could increase his capital holding to equal that of his partners and consequently equalise profit sharing. This clause would become the cause of much discord between the partners before the first two years were concluded.

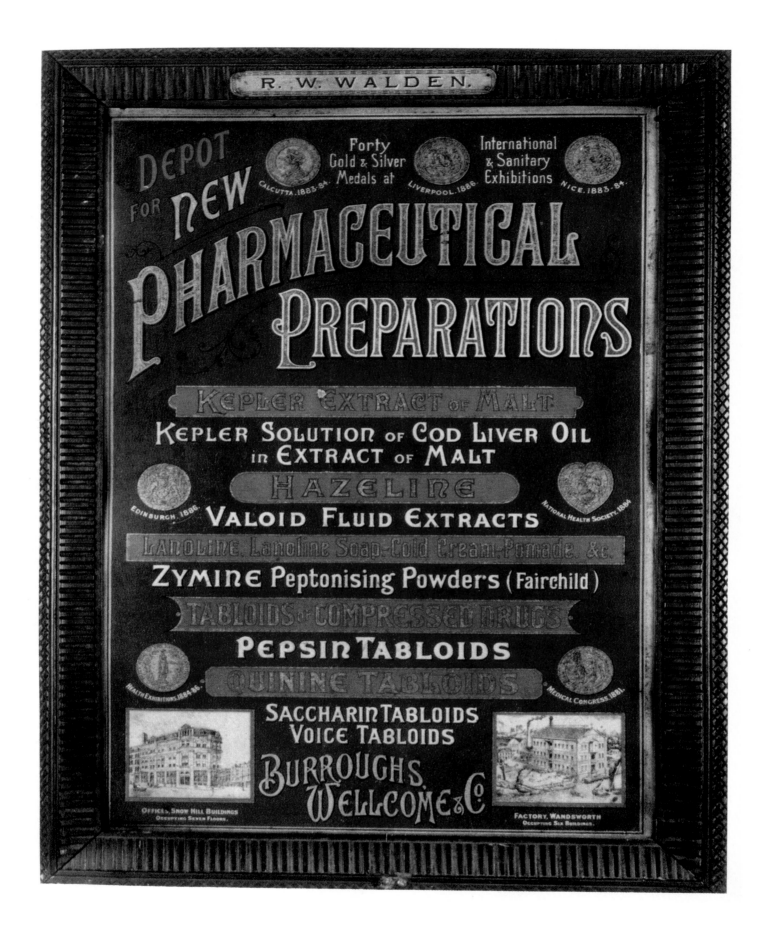

Above | A pharmacy sign from c. 1885 advertising Burroughs Wellcome & Co.'s product | Transatlantic Business   47

International Medical and Sanitary Exhibition
London, 1881

The headline banner reads "American Improvements In Pharmacy. Burroughs Wellcome & Co, 7 Snow Hill, London. Importers, Exporters and Manufacturing Chemists".

The spectacular presentation of mainly McKesson and Robbins and John Wyeth products was typical of their American companies of origin. However, the carefully designed packaging of pharmaceutical preparations was unusual in Victorian England and caused great excitement.

This particular exhibit, included the fullest range of products which both Burroughs and Wellcome could muster. The display, designed personally by Henry Wellcome, caused quite a stir amongst the visitors to the Exhibition.

The high standard of presentation became synonymous with the Burroughs Wellcome brand. As a result, awards and medals were presented to the company at exhibitions throughout Europe, including Milan and Stockholm. The partnership had been well and truly launched.

1883, Family Matters

It is generally acknowledged that Henry Wellcome's response to the news of Silas Burrough's proposed engagement to Olive Chase was extraordinarily negative. The announcement of Burrough's intentions evoked a churlish response from Wellcome. This is evident in the correspondence of early 1883. It would seem that Wellcome took this momentous opportunity to appraise Burrough's character, beyond a point normally expected of a friend and business colleague.

Perhaps Burrough's world tour, and the strain of holding the reins of the expanding business caused Wellcome to over react to the change in circumstance of his partner. Or, perhaps, Wellcome's fears of never finding personal fulfillment beyond his solitary circumstances caused him to respond in the way he did. Wellcome's patronising attitude, must have engendered a resentment not only in Silas Burroughs, but also in his intended wife, Olive. It seems more than likely that this tragic episode fuelled what was to be a prolonged feud between the partners over the running and control of the business. A pattern of disagreements and reconciliations would emerge alongside mutual company expansion goals beyond this date.

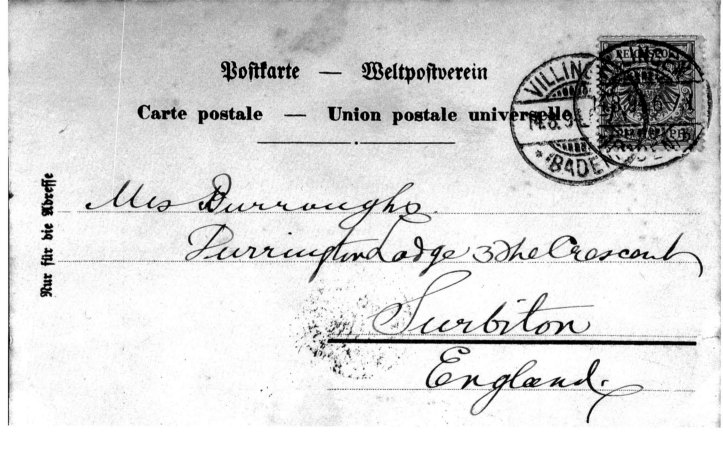

International Headquarters

On the 4th March 1883, Henry Wellcome informed his partner Silas Burroughs of the acquisition of a new corporate headquarters. Burroughs was on the other side of the world engaged in the Australasia leg of his business expansion tour. Occupying a prime position at the corner of Snow Hill and Holborn Viaduct, the radiused frontage of the building was an architectural manifestation of the partnership's ambitions. The 21 year lease carried a rent of £900 for the first year and £1,245 p.a. for the remainder. The acquisition was made only days after Wellcome had completed the Wandsworth factory fit-out and started production in earnest. Wellcome personally designed the interiors which were fitted under the direction of Dr. Christopher Dresser, art decorator of Sutton. Carved American walnut, plate glass and hammered copper lettering dominated the interior facades. The ground floor was mosaic. An American Eagle and a bronze replica Statue of Liberty overlooked the main suite. The rooms above were served by a spiral staircase and a goods lift. (See Wellcome's Legacy for further images).

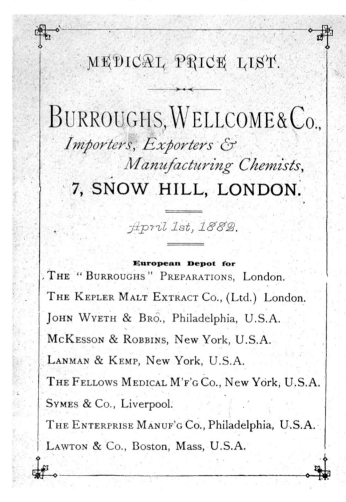

World's Columbian Exposition, Chicago 1893

The World's Columbian Exposition (World's Fair) celebrated the 400th anniversary of European man's arrival in the New World in 1492. The success of this World's Fair was due in no small way to the ambition of Chicago's leading commercial entrepreneurs led by the the very able second generation German immigrant, project director Charles H Wacker.

The Exhibition ran from May 1st to October 30th 1893 and was a remarkable achievement for the City of Chicago as only twenty-two years had elapsed since the great fire of 1871 had destroyed around four hundred acres of the city. Chicago's over reliance on timber plank for the construction of its buildings, roads and elevated sidewalks had proved catastrophic. Drought, and strong South Westerly winds had combined to ensure that the initial blaze became a firestorm resulting in the tragic death of two to three hundred citizens.

The World's Fair was situated on approximately six hundred acres of the previously desolate Jackson Park and Midway Plaisance. The two hundred or so new buildings of Beaux-Arts Architecture were linked by wide boulevards, canals and lagoons created by Frederick Law Olmsted in the French Classical style. The scale and grandeur of the architecture far exceeded any expectations and had a profound effect on American industrial optimism. Forty-six nations constructed exhibits for display in the Fair's impressive pavilions.

The most notable International pavilion contained exhibits from the emerging electricity industry. Commercial exhibits provided by Eddison, Western Electric and Westinghouse demonstrated the harnessing of alternating current. The Fair's buildings and boulevards were spectacularly illuminated by the Westinghouse designed light bulbs, following a competetive tendering process organised by the Fair's director.

Other attractions included the John Bull locomotive which was built in 1831, and had arrived triumphantly at the fair under its own steam. George Ferris constructed the first Big Wheel. Sixty people seated in thirty-six cars were rotationally elevated to 240 feet above the ground, affording spectacular views of the whole site.

Henry Wellcome, returning to Chicago to exhibit the developed product range of Burroughs Wellcome, must have been exhilarated by the achievements of Chicago's commercial and industrial magnates. Wellcome had first entered the city on May 1st 1872 in the aftermath of the fire. Wellcome's partner Silas Burroughs attended the International Peace Congress as the delegate from London, lobbying for freedom of trade and the abolition of customs tariffs.

The Architect, Daniel Hudson Burnham, whilst leading the team which designed the neoclassical white stucco pavilions inspirationally exalted his charges to:

'Make no small plans as they have no power to stir the blood of man.'

The Burroughs Wellcome partnership, despite the trials of the last thirteen years, must have been greatly inspired in Chicago. The 1893 World's Fair was undoubtably the catalyst for growth required after a decade of doubts and disputes. On a neighbouring plot, just outside the fairgrounds, Buffalo Bill Cody set up his famous Wild West Show, cashing in on the visitor numbers attending the World's Fair. This pastiche of the authentic Wild West which Wellcome had grown up in, also found its way into the colourful product marketing at the Burroughs Wellcome exhibition stand. This developing design flair and creativity, fuelled in Chicago's White City, would become a key element of the company business strategy in the years ahead.

INTERNATIONAL PEACE CONGRESS,
CHICAGO, 1893.

Proposition by S. M. Burroughs,
Delegate from the International Peace and Arbitration Society, London.

USTOMS Tariffs cause unfriendly feelings between states and nations. Freedom of trade tends to bring states and nations together in bonds of mutual interest, prosperity, friendship, and peace.

The general adoption of free trade would powerfully aid in preventing war by making peace a matter of common and universal interest.

Taxation, which restricts industry on the one hand, and creates special privileges on the other, tends to poverty of the industrial classes and builds up an aristocracy upon unearned wealth. It tends to social discontent, leading perhaps to violations of the peace.

The single tax on land values created by the

Influence and Explorers

> "There was a cockroach larger than a black beetle in the bathroom, there were no mosquito rods with the camp beds, my medical outfit which cost me four pounds ten at Burroughs Wellcome, had been left behind...."
>
> **Graham Greene, Journey Without Maps (1936)**

When Graham Greene embarked on his journey across Liberia in 1935 with his cousin Barbara, they formed yet another link in the long chain of explorers and adventurers relying upon a Burroughs Wellcome medical kit as an essential part of their expedition requirements. Greene's trek, undertaken a year after Sir Henry Wellcome's death, is redolent of the experiences of his predecessors who had penetrated Africa in the late 19th and early 20th centuries. In Kailahun, Greene remarks upon an encounter with a German traveller who was wearing a topee and carrying an ivory headed stick. Later in the journey, crossing from Sierra Leone into the Republic of Liberia, the nameless German was observed bobbing above the heads of his carriers, progressing effortlessly through the customs post on a chair slung between poles. This hammock chair, still being used as a method of bush transport in 1935, was an inferior version of the palanquin designed by Henry Wellcome for his fellow American, Mrs. May French Sheldon. This celebrated palanquin, occasionally containing Mrs. Sheldon, was carried by four Zanzibari porters. Mrs. French Sheldon's expedition through East Africa (1890 to 1891) was also the second expedition to carry the carefully designed and constructed Burroughs Wellcome medicine kit. This kit was a predecessor of the one that Graham Greene had lamentably left behind in 1935.

The first Burroughs Wellcome medical case was designed for the expedition to "rescue" Emin Pasha, Governor of Equatoria. This expedition (1887-1889) was led by Henry Morton Stanley, accompanied by Arthur Jeremy Mounteney Jephson. It was Wellcome's friendship with May Sheldon which cemented his relationship with Stanley and Jephson. Wellcome's network of friends in the field of exploration afforded him a great opportunity to promote the products of Burroughs Wellcome. He supplied these early expeditions with the tabloid medical kits free of charge, in the hope that the publicity generated would eventually reflect favourably on the Burroughs Wellcome tabloid brand. Henry Wellcome enthusiastically combined his interest in travel, exploration and the 'great outdoors' with the promotion of his company and its range of products. This instinct would distinguish him as a pioneer of advertising by association, where a brand becomes synonymous with supposedly heroic or sporting figures.

The following pages reveal a procession of adventurers who would not leave base camp without a custom designed Burroughs Wellcome tabloid medicine kit. Donated free of charge, they could be dismissed as merely marketing ploys. However, close examination of the succession of kits reveals a meticulous design philosophy. The challenges faced by Arctic and Antarctic explorers were very different to those faced by aviators and Amazonian anthropologists. Generic designs would not suffice. Task specific design, combined with Wellcome's sound belief in research and quality control are clearly evident in the various expedition supplies. Wellcome was clearly ahead of his time in this field. Strong brand association with adventurers is still evident in the 21st century, as exemplified by Sir Richard Branson's Virgin brand sponsorship of the late aviator and balloonist Steve Fossett. Although Wellcome attempted to steer clear of the myriad political issues of the late 19th century, his continued loyalty to his close friends, Henry Stanley and May French Sheldon, would at times put him at odds with his business partner Silas Burroughs, who kept very different company.

Sir Henry Morton Stanley and the Quest, Rescue and Retreat of Emin, Governor of Equatoria

In 1882 Egypt became a British Protectorate. The insurgency that followed resulted in the capture of Khartoum in 1885 by Mahdist forces. As a consequence, the British-Egyptian administration of the Sudan and its southern province Equatoria disintegrated. The Governor of Equatoria, Emin Pasha became isolated in this vast remote region. Businessmen with colonial interests became concerned that Emin Pasha might meet the same fate as General Gordon in Khartoum. William Mckinnon and J. F. Hutton organised the "Emin Pasha Relief Committee" and approached H. M. Stanley to lead a privately funded relief expedition. Stanley readily agreed, and went to meet his employer King Leopold II of Belgium in Brussels to discuss the logistics. Stanley's ultimately flawed strategy, that of accessing Equatoria via the Congo and Aruwimi rivers, was primarily dictated by King Leopold's promised provision of Congo river boat steamers for shipping the expedition's substantial provisions.

EMIN PASHA.

anxious about Henry M Stanleys reported capture by the Mahdi or assassination by the natives in Africa—but hopeful we now have tidings which seem to prove that he is safe & will return to us again — the autographed portrait you have of him has one of the last signatures he wrote before leaving America & the portrait is an excellent one — He is noble hero & the world can illy afford to lose such men — with love & merry christmas & happy new year to you all I am always your affectionate

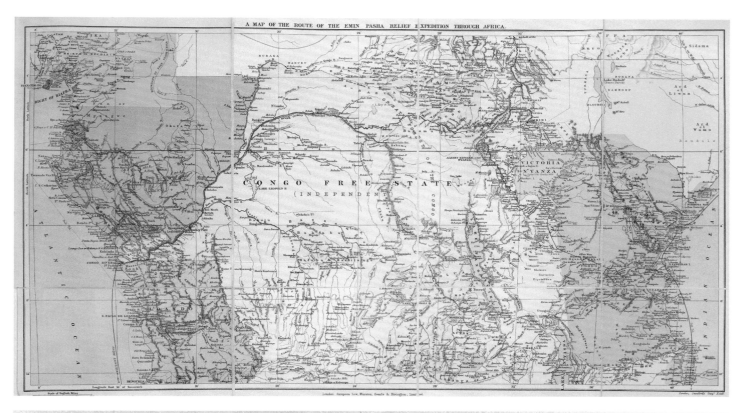

A MAP OF THE ROUTE OF THE EMIN PASHA RELIEF EXPEDITION THROUGH AFRICA.

SURGEON T. H. PARKE, A.M.D.   CAPTAIN NELSON.   H. M. STANLEY.   A. J. MOUNTENEY JEPHSON.

LIEUT. W. G. STAIRS, R.E.

Stanley, acting for McKinnon, also struck a deal with the Sultan of Zanzibar. This deal granted concessions to the Imperial British East Africa Company. The deal included the provision of the expedition carriers. The prospect of extracting a 75 ton ivory stockpile from Equatoria incentivised all parties, with the possible exception of the carriers. However, when Stanley arrived in Leopoldville in April 1887 the promised flotilla of steamers stood at only one river worthy boat, forcing Stanley to requisition a further two steamers and a barge from protesting missionaries.

The transport was inadequate for the expeditions logistical needs, many stores were abandoned and Stanley ordered the expedition to be split into an Advance and a Rear Column. Food was always in short supply for both columns, totalling approximately 1,000 men, and the impact on the villages along the route was resented, particularly at Yambuya, which was taken over and fortified by the advanced column.

This column, after 12 months and several sorties back and forth eventually arrived on the shores of Lake Albert. Here they assembled the 12 section steel boat, aptly named the Advance. Mounteney Jephson piloted the boat up to Mswa where he met with Emin Pasha on the 27th April 1888. Two days later Emin brought his steamer to the south end of the lake where he met with Stanley. Emin was able to supply Stanley's advanced expedition with food and assured Stanley that he had no intention of leaving the territory of Equatoria. Emin's primary need was for a supply of ammunition to defend the province, however the bulk of Stanley's ammunition and other stores had been left back in the Congo. Emins group of Egyptian soldiers and followers were arguably better positioned than those who had come to "rescue" them. Stanley retreated back down the trail to find the rear column. He found Bonny as the only remaining European in charge of the starving group decimated by sickness and desertion. Eventually, in early 1889 the remnants of Stanley's expedition and Emin's soldiers and their families converged above Lake Albert. A fairly disunited trek through East Africa to the coast ensued. The groups eventually dispersed via Zanzibar back to Cairo. Stanley's expedition account "In Darkest Africa" accused Bartellot and Jameson of incompetence in leading the rear column. This expedition was also noted as the first to carry the newly developed Maxim machine gun into Africa.

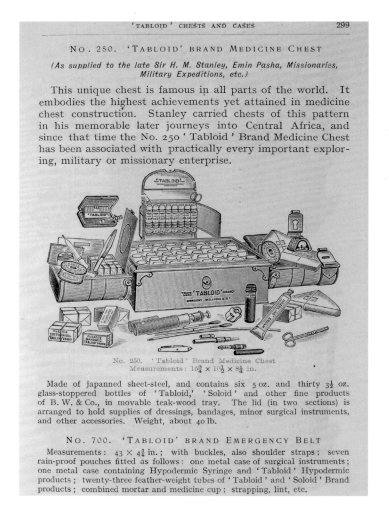

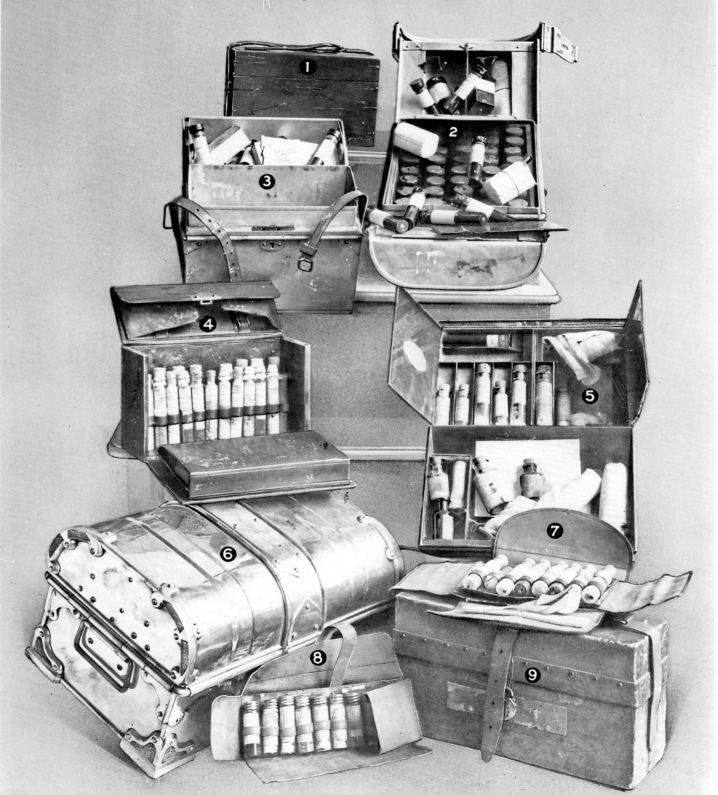

Burroughs Wellcome & Co. (1934) The romance of exploration and emergency first-aid from Stanley to Byrd: New York

The Thanksgiving Day Banquet of 1896

Silas Burrough's premature death in 1895 left Henry Wellcome at the head of the growing worldwide pharmaceutical business. Wellcome had now mainly resided in London for the last fifteen years, enjoying all that the capital had to offer. Wellcome had been introduced to the Order of Free Masons by his general manager Robert Sudlow in 1885, and had risen through its ranks to become influential among the well connected members of its masculine society. Henry Wellcome's friends, both male and female, could have been forgiven for assuming that Henry at the age of 43 was a confirmed bachelor. This lifestyle was not considered unusual for a dedicated businessman at the time. By November 1896, Wellcome was chairman of London's American Association, probably the zenith of his social standing in Victorian society. This prestigious position allowed Wellcome to take 'centre stage' during a Thanksgiving banquet attended by the most influential Anglo Americans including H. M. Stanley, Mounteney Jephson and Hiram S. Maxim.

Mr Passmore Edwards.

Mr T Walter Earle (Hon. Secretary)

Mr Newton Crane (Vice Chairman)

Mr A.J. Mounteney Jephson

Miss Florence K Upton

ebsler P.

dy Lockwood

Mr Wellcome. (Chairman)

Mrs H.M Stanley.

Sir Frank Lockwood Q.C M.P

A GROUP AT THE FEAST.

From an original drawing by Herbert Johnson

Mrs May French Sheldon

In the 21st century the cult of celebrity often describes those who are famous for being famous. In the late 19th century Mrs May French Sheldon's claim to fame stemmed from her taking a journey through East Africa in 1890. The purpose of the journey seems to have been simply to undertake a journey that no white woman had been reported as taking before. Visitors to the Chicago World's Fair in 1894 may well have questioned the motives of Mrs. Sheldon's publication, "Sultan to Sultan", which related the story of her travels. Dressed glamorously in a white ball gown, blonde wig and tiara it was unclear as to whom had discovered whom.

Of considerably more importance was French Sheldon's sojourn through the Congo Free State in 1903-1904 (without the celebrated palanquin). This trip was commissioned and financed by W. T. Stead, in his capacity as the London editor of the "Review of Reviews". The former editor of the "Pall Mall Gazette" was now engaged in investigations for what would later be revealed as the Congo Reform Association. W. T. Stead and his colleague E. D. Morel nurtured the naive belief that Mrs. French Sheldon would be viewed as a neutral observer in the mounting debate on the colonisation of Africa by the European powers. This view was taken regardless of the Sheldon's close friendship with Henry Morton Stanley who had been instrumental in supporting King Leopold II of Belgium's personal acquisition of the Congo Free State at the Berlin conference in 1885. Recently widowed, and with her celebrity and finances waning, Mrs. Sheldon readily accepted the secret commission from Stead. Mrs. Sheldon arrived in Africa in November 1903, well prepared by Stead to carry out a thorough investigation into reports of sytematic violent abuses of the native Congolese under the the rubber ravenous regime of King Leopold.

Upon her arrival May Sheldon was briefed by the British Consul, Roger Casement. Consul Casement had been posted in Boma since the turn of the century and was now preparing to return to England to deliver his own report on the Congo situation to the British Foreign Office in London.

The Casement report comprehensively detailed the atrocities perpetrated by Leopold's Congo companies. The report was specific in cataloguing the crimes including locations, dates and even the names of the perpetrators. King Leopold had been informed about the impending Casement report and made plans to counter its impact. Leopold's main strategy in dealing with the British was to threaten to hand over the territories under his personal command to Germany.

Mrs. FRENC

This palanquin was made at Whiteley's for Mr Henry S. Welcome (of Messrs. Burroughs & W work, and Mr. Wellcome must be congratulated

H SHELDON'S PALANQUIN.

French Sheldon, the "Lady Stanley" who is bound for Central Africa, from designs by **Mr.**
:llcome, Snow Hill). It is a unique specimen of strong, light, and artistic cane and bamboo
a his excellent taste. The palanquin will be carried by four of Mrs. Sheldon's Zanzibari porters.

Roger Casement 1864 - 1916

This threat was delivered to the British Foreign Office by Sir Alfred Jones, the consul for the Congo in Liverpool, who was also a director of the Compagnie Belge Maritime du Congo (a Leopold concessionaire company). The British response to Leopold's threat was to severely edit the report, deleting the specific references and all the named parties. Parliamentary under-secretary Lord Percy also exerted pressure on the Foreign Office to dilute the report and seek verification of its contents via an International Commission. Casement was naturally livid at this juncture. Although the appointments of the commission members were also influenced by Leopold, the Casement report was fully vindicated by the commission in February 1905. As for Mrs Sheldon, while the report of the International Commission was pending, she wrote a letter to The Times dismissing the reports of brutality. The letter and subsequent Sheldon lectures praised the Belgian monarch's efforts in instilling the discipline of work as a civilising influence upon a lazy and inept native black population. Mrs. Sheldons role as an apologist for King Leopold's tyrannical regime continued for many years alongside her own colonial ambitions. Consequently it would take another four years for the Belgian Government to remove the Congo Free State from King Leopold's grasp in 1908, prior to his death in 1909.

In 1905 Casement was awarded a CMG (he did not open or acknowledge the honour). In 1906 he accepted the post as British Consul General in Rio de Janeiro, Brazil. On St. Patrick's day, March 17th 1911, Casement submitted a report to the Foreign Secretary detailing abuse of the Putamayo Indians by the British registered Peruvian Amazonian Company. Some of the front line hired enforcers named in Casement's report were brought to trial for murder in Peru, though the directors of the rubber company, Julio Cesar Arana and his brother escaped prosecution. Disillusioned with a lifetime spent representing what he now regarded as a duplicitous British consular service, Casement resigned his post in 1913, by now he was a Knight of the British Empire. Sir Roger then turned his attention towards the cause of his own native people. In August 1914, the feuding of Europe's monarchs degenerated into a devastating war. Sir Roger Casement, now working for the cause of Irish independence, travelled to Germany with the intention of establishing allies and securing arms for the 1916 Easter Rising. The tragic events that followed would result in Casement's, capture, imprisonment and trial for treason. Roger Casement was subsequently executed by the British government that he had diligently served for most of his remarkable life.

The South Pole

Right | Portrait of Sir Ernest Henry Shackleton

Below | Model of the S.S. Discovery, Captain Scott's ship. From the Natural History Museum, South Kensington

Opposite Page Top and Bottom | Tabloid first aid super pocket kit, with a waterproof canvas cover, by Burroughs Wellcome & Co (USA) Inc.
The kit was used by Finn Ronne on the U.S. Antarctic expedition of 1939-1941. The case is displayed alongside its canvas cover.
His wife, Edith Ronne, accompanied him on this expedition, she served as a historian and correspondent for the North American Newspaper Alliance.
Edith Ronne and the chief pilot's wife, Jennie Darlington, were the first women to overwinter in Antarctica.
The underside of the case (Top) contains a detailed map of the expedition route.

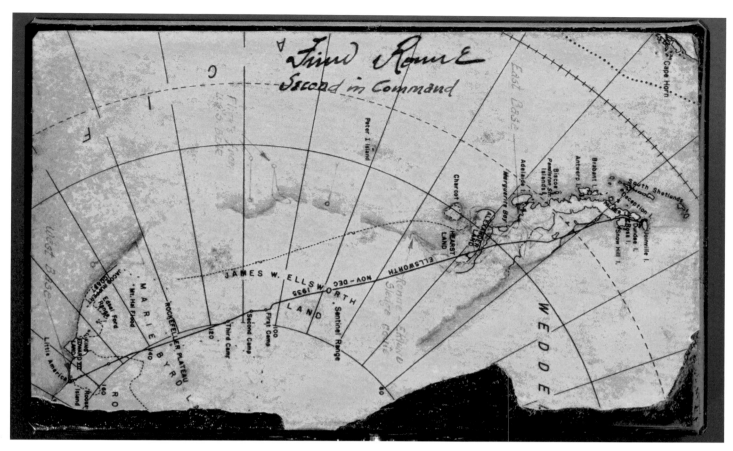

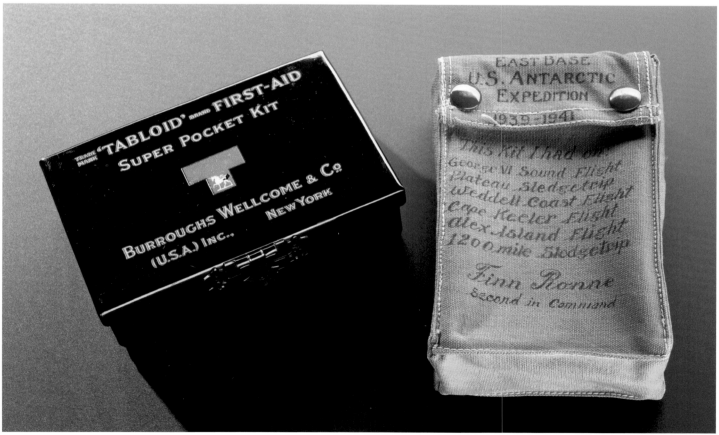

Antarctic Imagery

When Captain Robert Falcon Scott's ship, the Terra Nova embarked from Cardiff, Wales on the ill-fated British Antarctic Expedition in 1910, it was loaded with all manner of supplies including a Burroughs Wellcome tabloid medical chest. The expedition's official photographer Herbert Ponting, who was 40 years old at the time, joined the ship in New Zealand. As the first ever "camera artist" employed on an Antarctic expedition, Ponting was aware of the importance of the assignment that would come to dominate the remainder of his life. Ponting's previous work in the field of stereoscopic photography had culminated in the publication of "In Lotus-land Japan" in 1910. He had also been "Harpers Weekly" correspondent covering the Russo-Japanese war in 1904-5. Inevitably the tragic nature of the expedition with the deaths of Scott, Oates, Wilson, Bowers and Evans engendered a fascination for Ponting's photographic and moving images. His book, "The Great White South" published in 1921 was very successful. In 1933 the movie "Ninety Degrees South: With Scott to the Antarctic" opened to critical acclaim.

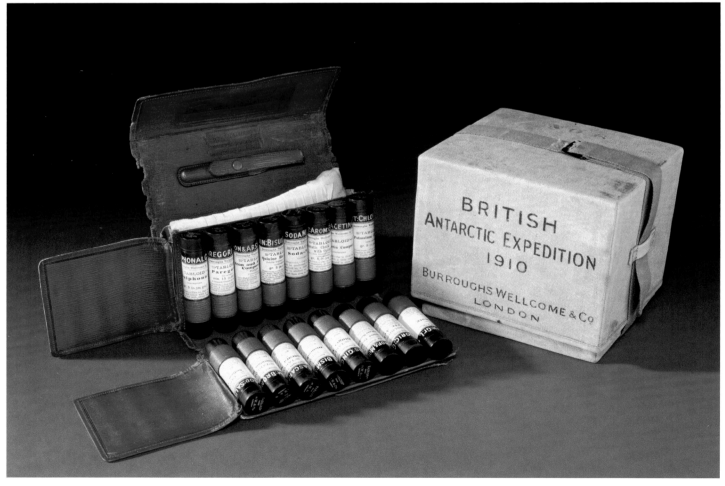

MR. H. G. PONTING, F.R.G.S., official photographer to the British Antarctic Expedition, 1910, developing a plate with 'TABLOID' 'RYTOL' in his dark-room in the hut at the winter quarters, Cape Evans.

CAPTAIN SCOTT

And members of the Southern Party, British Antarctic Expedition, at their camp, twenty miles from Mount Erebus.

Negative developed with 'TABLOID' 'RYTOL' on the spot. Print toned with

'TABLOID' BLUE TONER

The Aviators

Below | The first aid kit was used on the first transatlantic flight by airship, in July 1919. The British team flew to New York from England and returned within 183 hours. The kit also contains a booklet on first aid, although the second half of the book advertises other Tabloid chests.

Below Right | Tabloid kit was used on the first non-stop transatlantic flight on 14-15 June 1919 by Sir Arthur Whitten Brown (1886-1948) and Sir John William Alcock (1892-1919). Alcock and Brown completed the treacherous crossing in 16 hours 27 minutes. The flight was a matter of national prestige. The men shared the £10,000 prize from the Daily Mail, which had been set up to encourage British aviation. The kit contained bandages, dressings, cotton wool, court plaster, and drugs for pain relief, upset stomachs, nausea, and antiseptics. It also contained carron oil made from linseed oil and lime water for burns and scalds, which were among the most likely injuries on an aircraft full of hot metal; in fact the tube is half empty.

Opposite Page Top | This medicine chest was used by Walter Wellmann (1858-1934) and Melvin Vaniman (1866 - 1912) during their attempt to cross the Atlantic Ocean in a powered airship called America in September 1910. Their journey was unsuccessful. Vaniman died on his second attempt, in 1912, when his airship exploded

Opposite Page Bottom | This case was given to one of the four two-man crews on the first circumnavigation of the globe by air by the US Army Air Service World Flight in 1924. The case was presented back to Burroughs, Wellcome & Co and signed as a memento by the six airmen in the successful Boston, Chicago and Seattle planes. The trip took an incredible 175 days.

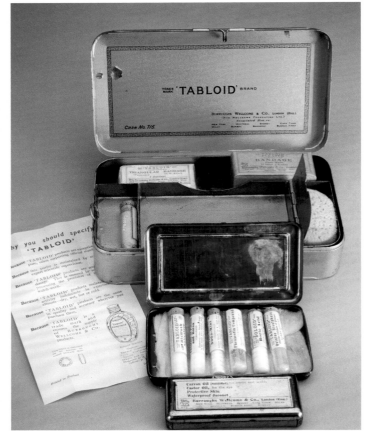

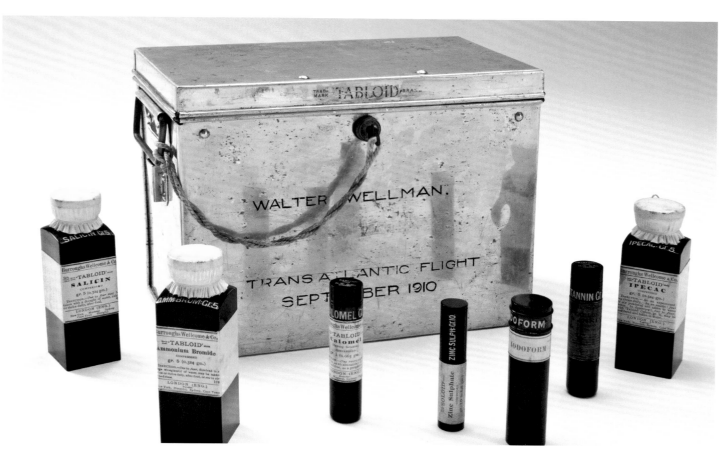

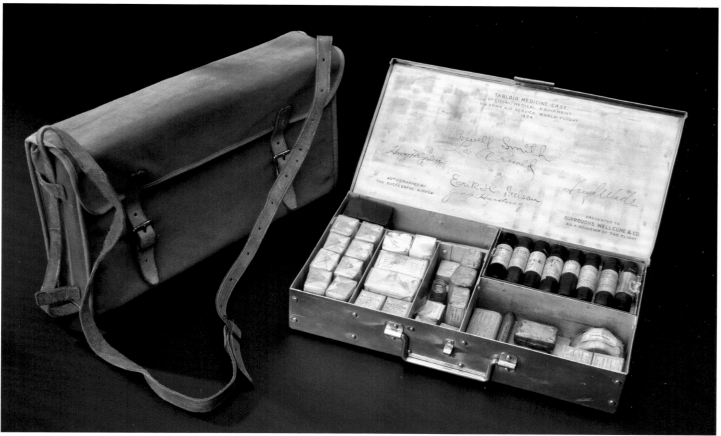

Empires and the Sudan

"The empires of the future are the empires of the mind"

Winston Churchill

When General Gordon was killed at the hands of the Mahdi's army in Khartoum in 1885, it was perceived in Britain as a serious affront to the Empire of Queen Victoria. The years that followed were considered, by the British, to be disastrous for the Sudanese people who lived under the rule of the Mahdi, and his successor Khalifa Abdallahi.

It would take a period of thirteen years or so, and a change of government in London, before the British army under the command of General Herbert Kitchener, would be able to rout the Dervish army at Omduraman close to Khartoum and claim Sudan for the Crown. The year was 1898, and Kitchener was hailed as a national hero. Gordon's death had been avenged and British pride restored.

The initiative for the victorious campaign came as a direct result of the political influence of Evelyn Baring (Lord Cromer) over the Colonial Office of Joseph Chamberlain. However, it would be the post campaign vision of Kitchener entitled "Civilisation after Conquest" that would fire the enthusiasm of Henry Wellcome and draw him to Khartoum.

 Kitchener appealed to the public of Great Britain to back his plan to educate the people of the Sudan and free them from the famine and disease exacerbated by the long wars fought in their country. Wellcome had always taken a keen interest in the welfare of the indigenous populations of both the American and British Empires.

Henry Wellcome responded to this humanitarian appeal by immediately donating 100 guineas and a stock of medical equipment. This donation would become part of the project to build a college in Khartoum in the name and memory of General Gordon. When Wellcome embarked upon the journey to Cairo in the autumn of 1900, it would initiate his company's pioneering work in the field of tropical medicine. In 1901 the Wellcome Tropical Research laboratories were opened in Khartoum. In the same year the appearance of Syrie Barnado in this landscape would also set a further chapter of Henry Wellcome's life in motion, as Henry and Syrie were married on 25th June, 1901 (See For Better or Worse).

Almost ten years would elapse before Wellcome returned alone to Khartoum, recently estranged from his young wife. The 1910 winter in Egypt and Sudan was another recommended convalescence in Wellcome's recovery from a serious illness. Prior to his solitary departure from England, Wellcome had visited Lord Kitchener who implored him again to come to the aid of the people of Sudan. Henry Wellcome clearly gave Kitchener's request considerable thought, and, by the time he had reached Khartoum he had formulated the idea of providing work for the native population by means of an archaeological project. This welfare work project would also afford Wellcome an opportunity to seriously develop his interest in archaeology and anthropology.

The boulders released from their resting places in Jebel Moya in the years from 1910 to 1914 would serve not only to enliven the venture, but would also trap Henry Wellcome in a quest for historical artifacts that would defy assessment for a further thirty-five years. Frank Addison, in the Jebel Moya text published in 1949, was eventually able to appraise the archaeological work following the interventions of World War I, Wellcomes death in 1936 and World War II. The enormous volume of material shipped to London from the Sudan excavations were finally rationalised and displayed at the Wellcome Centenary Exhibition in 1953.

THE KITCHENER MEMORIAL MEDICAL SCHOOL. KHARTOUM.

Mr. G. B. Bridgman, A.R.I.B.A., Architect.

THE BUILDER—JANUARY 4, 192

Sir Andrew Balfour

The British Medical Journal obituary notice of February 7th 1931 reported the death of "Balfour of Khartum...man of a thousand friends". At the time of his death, Edinburgh born Balfour was director of the London School of Hygiene and Tropical Medicine. Balfour's career was a relentless pursuit in the cause of public health and the prevention of disease. Following service in the Boer War as a civil surgeon, Balfour became director of the Wellcome Tropical Research Laboratory, Khartoum in 1902 at the age of 29. He would remain in Khartoum until 1913 as medical officer of health advising the Sudanese government. His achievements in sanitising the city and, in particular, the precinct of Khalifa defined his career. In the European quarter of Khartoum, Balfour's antimalarial measures became so effective that he introduced a 10 shilling fine if a live insect was discovered in staff quarters. Legend has it that he imposed the first fine upon himself when inspectors found that a solitary mosquito had managed to invade Balfour's own residence.

In 1914 Balfour found himself once again in military service.

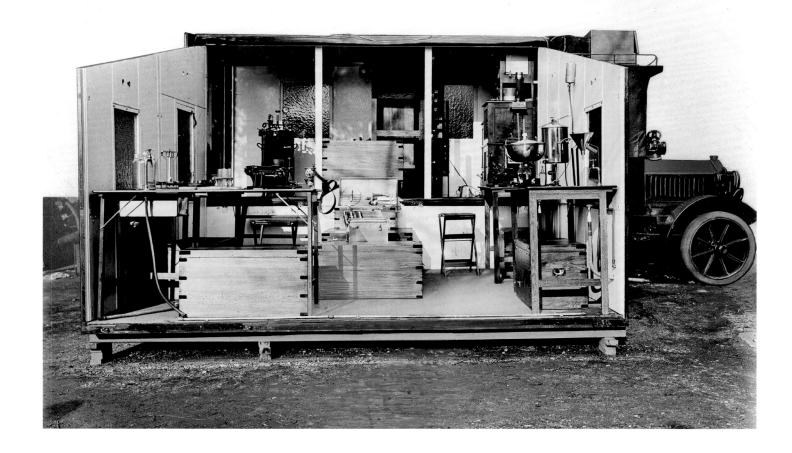

Charles Morley Wenyon

Serving alongside Dr. Balfour was Dr. Charles Morley Wenyon who had joined the Wellcome Bureau of Scientific Research from the London School of Tropical Medicine only a few months before the outbreak of World War I. As a protozoologist, Wenyon's experience in the Sudan in 1906 and 1907 was invaluable to the armed forces fighting in the Middle East. His contributions to the publications, "Human intestinal Protozoa in the Near East" and "Memorandum on Medical Diseases in Tropical and Subtropical Areas" were published by the Army Council. Wenyon then turned his attention to the plight of the malaria stricken Allied Forces in Salonica. This work would occupy him beyond 1918. He eventually returned to the Wellcome Bureau of Scientific Research in 1920, succeeding Balfour as director in 1923. Under Wenyon's directorship the Bureau became internationally renowned. In 1945 Wenyon was elected as President of the Royal Society of Tropical Medicine, he received the Society's prestigious Manson medal in 1947.

As a result of Wenyon's continued interest in malaria in the Balkan's, the work of Dr. Henry Foy's laboratory gained support from the Wellcome Trust. (See Wellcome's Legacy.).

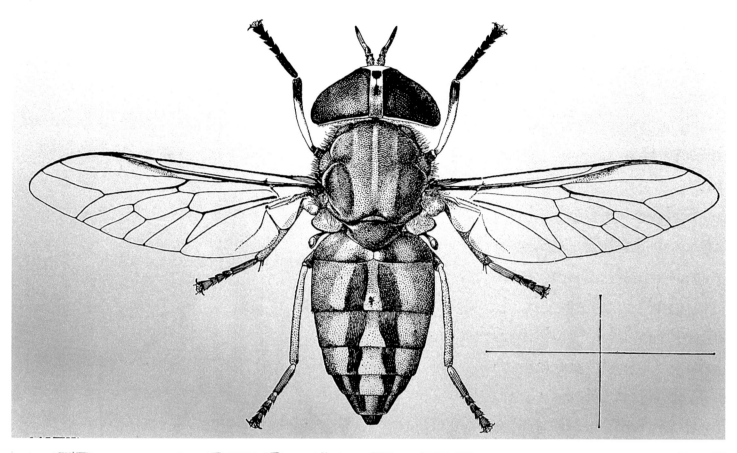

Above | Interior of the Culex floating laboratory on the Nile, Sudan | Empires and the Sudan 87

Jebel Moya

The use of aerial photography in archaeology can reveal tell tale traces of long since buried structures and signs of previous habitation. Earth mapping is now carried out using aircraft mounted cameras, or from earth orbiting satellites. However, before the age of the plane improvised methods of elevating cameras were used to great effect.

The remarkable photographs in the Wellcome Collection reveal a great deal about Wellcome's experiments with cameras raised into the air with the aid of cables and kites. While these devices would only reveal what was already apparent from the ground, they did produce images recording the areas excavated from otherwise inaccessible angles.

Jebel Moya Volume 1, Frank Addison, Oxford University Press 1949 describes how Henry Wellcome's archaeological enterprise was undertaken primarily to provide meaningful work for the benefit of the native population. Addison describes this neatly, "Archaeology, in short, was the handmaid of philanthropy. Wellcome believed he had discovered a "prehistoric site", the home of an ancient white race. Enlisting the help of Governor General Sir Reginald Wingate he applied for excavation permits in January 1911.

Above | View of the excavated remains of the ancient Christian church at Seqadi | Empires and the Sudan 89

Jebel Moya

The site, lying between the Blue and White Nile rivers in the southern Gezira plain, was at the time considered remote from the Khartoum administration. Two years before Wellcome's arrival, Mr. Scott Moncrief had been killed in the "Wad Haboba" rising in the Gezira. As a result, when the Jebel Moya camp was established, Wellcome ran the camp in a military fashion. A clause inserted in the excavation licence empowered him to maintain armed guards for the protection of the European camp personnel who resided in aligned tents. The native workforce were housed in grass huts (tukls) lower down the valley. The working day was regulated by bugle calls.

While at first the native population were at best indifferent, and at worst hostile, to the enterprise on their doorstep, the wages on offer provided the incentive for the work force to grow from less than twenty to around 500 men and boys in the three winter seasons of excavation prior to World War I. While Henry Wellcome was personally directing operations at the site, he relied upon the advice of Dr. Reisner who recommended the professional archaeological staff for the project. As a result Mr. Oric Bates took charge of excavations while Dr. Douglas Derry became the site anthropologist and the camp Medical Officer for the second season. Oric Bates soon discovered that the site was a huge graveyard requiring a change of excavation methods.

While archaeological staff and anthropologists came and went with the seasons, Henry Wellcome needed a trusted, reliable man to coordinate the project and protect his interests in the region. That man was Major J. S. Uribe who maintained the Jebel Moya site on behalf of Wellcome from 1911 until April 1938 when the site reverted back to the Sudan government. When Wellcome was in Quito, Ecuador in 1909 en route to the Panama Canal zone he had met Major Uribe through American Government delegates. Uribe was at odds with the Ecuadorian regime and with Wellcome's help became exiled from Ecuador. It cannot be confirmed that Wellcome saved the Major from a firing squad, however Major Uribe became Henry Wellcomes right hand man in the Sudan. The Major demonstrated extraordinary loyalty up to and beyond Wellcome's death in 1936. Major Uribe and his family were duly rewarded by a provision made in Sir Henry's will.

Above | H. Wellcome and his medical officer Dr Ray with a party of Sheiks, Seqadi, 1913 | Empires and the Sudan

Empires and the Sudan | **Above | H. S. Wellcome with the Sultans of Socota, Jebel Moya**

Major Uribe and The House of Boulders

Frank Addison acknowledges Major Uribe's contribution to his report in describing the varied activities and developments in the Jebel Moya camp and the nearby village.

As the work of the archaeologists became more measured due to the huge numbers of graves encountered on the site, the excess labour was put to work building a huge "stone age" style structure. The House of Boulders would eventually house Major Uribe for many years, along with a dispensary that would serve the needs of Jebel Moya until 1938.

Wellcome's welfare work even extended to lifestyle choices for his native workers with the introduction of a savings bank. Sustained abstinence from the local alcoholic brew, merrisa, was rewarded with the ceremonial Order of the Peacock feather. Other accrued benefits of the project included a school, improved housing, a mosque and agricultural development adjacent to the Blue Nile near Sennar.

Addison reports the great lengths that Wellcome went to with continued support for the welfare of the Sudanese. In 1934 he brought fish from Florida that devour mosquito larvae. These "gambusia" were then taken to Sudan by Major Uribe to help with the fight against malaria.

The Panama Survey, 1909

In the words of Theodore Roosevelt:

"A finer body of men has never been gathered by any nation than the men who have done the work of building the Panama Canal. The conditions under which they have lived and done their work have been better than in any similar work ever undertaken in the tropics. They have all felt an eager pride in their work, and they have made not only America but the whole world their debtors by what they have accomplished". In 1909, as a result of the reputation of the Wellcome Tropical Research Laboratory in Khartoum, Henry Wellcome was requested by the American Secretary of War, J. M. Dickinson to undertake a survey of the conditions for workers in the Panama Canal Zone. In Panama, Wellcome endorsed the work of William Crawford Gorgas who was chief sanitary officer on the canal project. Gorgas's measures were vital to the success of the project and included draining swamps, fumigating and protecting the workers living quarters with mosquito netting, significantly reducing the incidences of yellow fever and malaria. Previously, in Havana, Gorgas had capitalised on the work of Cuban doctor Carlos Finlay. Gorgas is seated next to 1902 Nobel Prize winner Sir Ronald Ross in the image below. The empty chair next to Henry Clay Weeks may have been vacated by the unknown photographer.

Next Pages:

Left Top | Panama Canal construction workers arriving at the Gorgona train station, 1910

Left Bottom | Panama Canal, construction workers of Italian origin. Juan Grande, 1910

Right Top | Panama Canal, sleeping quarters for European labourers, interior showing fold-up bunks, 1911

Right Bottom | Panama Canal construction workers (American and European) dining in the Isthmian Canal Commission Hotel, Culebra, Panama 1910

Above | W. C. Gorgas (left), Sir Ronald Ross (centre) and Henry Clay Weeks

Above | Pedro Miguel Locks, Panama Canal looking south from east, 1910 | Empires and the Sudan

For Better or Worse

"The men that women marry, and why they marry them, will always be a marvel and a mystery to the world."

Michael Angelo

1901 marked the end of the Victorian era. On the 22nd of January, a stunned Prince of Wales, became King Edward VII, following the death of his mother Queen Victoria who had reigned imperiously for 63 years. The new century also marked the end of an era for Henry Wellcome, who, at the age of forty-seven, was considered by most of his friends and associates to be a confirmed bachelor. However, when twenty-two year old Syrie Barnado arrived in the Sudan in the spring of 1901, the existing friendship between them inexplicably spiraled into a full blown 'whirlwind romance'. In Michael Ondaatje's novel, the 'English Patient', Almasy's journal refers to "the haboob, a Sudan dust storm that dresses in bright yellow walls a thousand metres high and is followed by rain". The intense feelings stirred in both Henry and Syrie during this 'chance encounter' may well have been fanned by the desert winds as the courtship rapidly developed into an engagement to be married. The momentous speed of events appear to be particularly out of character for a mature man who had been very sceptical on the subject of matrimony in earlier correspondence. Hearty congratulations were forthcoming from Wellcome's closest friends, most notably a tragically prophetic letter written by Mounteney Jephson. Wellcome received the letter on the 4th June 1901, and would have read the following. "I recognise that you are a person who would be made or marred by marriage - one might say that of many people, but it is more true of you than anyone I know". Mr. Henry S. Wellcome married Gwendoline Maude Syrie Barnado on Tuesday, 25th June 1901, at St. Mark's Church Surbiton. Wellcome's best man was his loyal friend Jephson who was still suffering the after effects of the African expedition he had undertaken with H. M. Stanley.

For the Wellcome's, settling into married life would simply be a case of Syrie, known as Queenie to her friends, adapting to the lifestyle of Henry Wellcome, known as Hal to his friends. This was the convention of the time. Social and political rights were still denied to women in 1901. It would be another two years before Mrs. Emmeline Pankhurst formed the militant campaigning suffragette group aimed primarily at gaining votes for women.

The Wellcome's lifestyle reflected that of an Edwardian gentleman of status and influence. Their first marital home, the Oast House in Hayes, Kent, was an elegant property with extensive grounds, built in 1873 by Lord Sackville Cecil, the half-brother of the third Marquis of Salisbury. It was here that they settled before leaving for Europe in September 1901. This eight month excursion would be the first of many. Burroughs Wellcome was an international business, and since the death of Silas Burroughs in 1895, Henry Wellcome was the chief ambassador for the business. This was not the age of the plane, The Wright brothers first flight did not occur until December 1903, and travelling could be prolonged and arduous.

On the 26th June 1903 Henry Mounteney Wellcome was born. The christening was held at St. Michael's, Chester Square and the reception at Claridge's Hotel, London. Henry and Syrie's son was named after his godfathers, the explorers, Sir Henry Morton Stanley and Mounteney Jephson.

On May 9th of the following year, Sir Stanley died at the age of 63. The planning and organisation of the funeral was carried out by Henry Wellcome in accordance with the deceased explorer's instructions. Stanley's greatest wish was to be buried next to Dr. David Livingstone in Westminster Abbey.

Hal and Queenie

Stanley's wish, unfortunately proved to be presumptuous, as the Dean of Westminster, Joseph Armitage Robinson forbade the internment in the Abbey, although the funeral service was held there. This incident was the cause of some distress to Henry Wellcome and the bereaved Lady Dorothy Stanley.

With this sad duty to his friend fulfilled, Henry Wellcome and his new family headed for North America in the autumn of 1904 until April 1905, firstly visiting the Wellcome family in Minnesota. The tour then moved on to Chicago, The World's Fair in St. Louis, Washington for the inauguration of President Roosevelt and finally Philadelphia. The business of attending prestigious functions and being feted by the American Medical Association being just reward for Wellcome's transatlantic business achievements. With his young, beautiful wife and his infant son alongside him, Henry Wellcome could have been forgiven for thinking that the trials and tribulations of his once solitary existence were at last behind him.

In September 1905, Syrie's father, Dr T. J. Barnado died at the age of sixty. Henry Wellcome diligently made all the arrangements for the funeral, which, in its grandeur, illustrated the high regard in which he held his father in law.

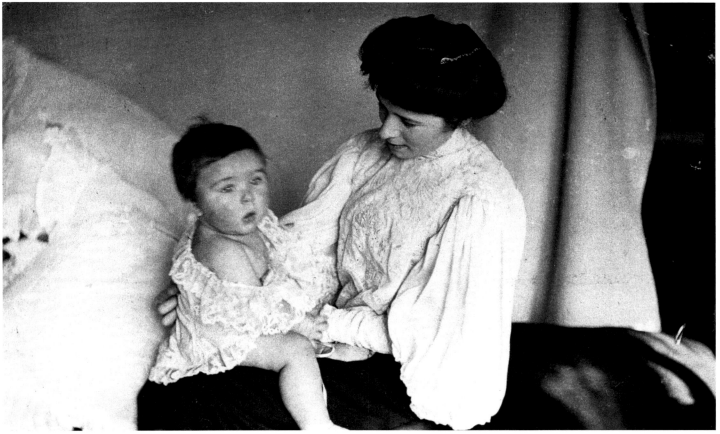

Gran Tourismo

In 1904 another union took place; that of Mr. Charles Rolls and Mr. Henry Royce, who reached an agreement at the Midland Hotel in Manchester. C. S. Rolls undertook to sell the cars of F. H. Royce under the name Rolls-Royce. The age of the motor car had arrived for the gentlemen of London who would embrace the freedom of the open, though somewhat bumpy roads of England and Continental Europe. Henry Wellcome, as an avid traveller, soon became enamoured with the new mode of transport. The ability to move freely without the constraints of rail would now allow him to further indulge in his joint passions of travelling and collecting. Wellcome's personal quest to stage an exhibition on the History of Medicine was already well under way, with agents deployed to search out artifacts for this purpose. The most notable agent at this stage being Dr. C. J. S. Thompson. The advent of the motor car also presented a further opportunity, specifically, the design and manufacture of Tabloid first-aid travellers kits customised for the motorist. The first cracks in the Wellcome's marriage may well have developed as a result of travelling those bumpy roads, as Wellcome's passions, were apparently not those of his young wife.

Below left | Mrs. Syrie Syrie Wellcome on board ship c. 1905 | Henry Wellcome's car on tour in Portugal c. 1906

Below Right | Mrs. Syrie Wellcome and Mounteney Wellcome on board ship c. 1905

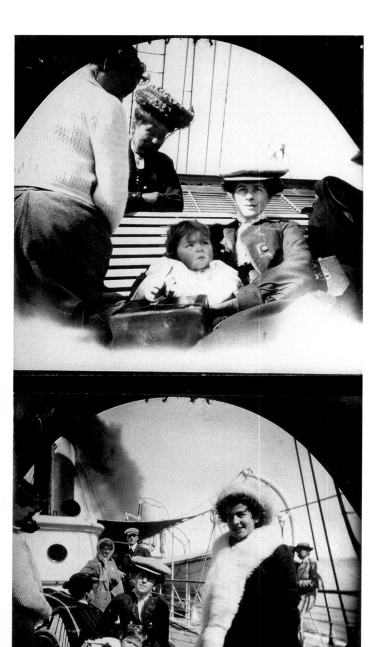

The Wellcomes At Home, and Abroad

Some of the most delightful images in the Wellcome Collection are those of Henry Wellcome, his wife Syrie and their son Mounteney. As family photographs, they illustrate the love and devotion that the family members obviously had for one another. The intimacy between mother and son, and father and son is evident in the images. The conventions of the era may have dictated, however the absence of intimacy in the few portraits of the couple together, may hold a clue as to, what can only be described as, the unfortunate disintegration of their marriage towards the end of 1909.

Right | The Oast House, Hayes, Kent. The first home of Henry and Syrie Wellcome

Below | Syrie Wellcome and Mounteney in Biarritz c. 1906

Below right | Sir Henry Wellcome and Mounteney c. 1915

Opposite below | Henry Wellcome and Mounteney Wellcome, holiday sports at The Mansion, Sunbridge Park, Kent 1913

Quito, Ecuador, 1909

From Autumn 1905 to May 1906 and throughout the winter of 1907-8 the Wellcome's travelled extensively by motor car throughout Southern Europe. This culminated in a sojourn to Lisbon, which unfortunately coincided with the assassination of King Carlos I, and his son, Crown Prince Luiz on February 1st, 1909. Rioting ensued in the capital of Portugal. These incidents, and the duration of the expeditions (generally six months) placed a great strain on the Wellcome's marriage as Syrie grew increasingly disenchanted with the seemingly endless, arduous, quest for "curios".

Reports also indicate that Wellcome's health was adversely affected by this nomadic lifestyle, so much so, that a recuperative holiday in California was deemed necessary in the fall of 1909. This cure would still require an Atlantic crossing to New York, and a train journey of 3,000 miles from the cold North Atlantic to the sunshine of the West Coast.

However the final straw which broke the Sudanese camel's back would be placed, unconsciously, by U.S. Secretary of War, J. M. Dickinson. On the return journey to New York, Wellcome was requested to stop over in Washington. It was here that he readily agreed to travel to the Panama Canal Zone. Dickinson had persuaded him to carry out a detailed survey of the conditions endured by the multitude of workers engaged in the civil engineering project that would revolutionize shipping. Henry Wellcome was compelled to rise to this challenge and engage himself with the work of General William C. Gorgas, whose strategies to control the tropical diseases contracted by the canal zone workers was under scrutiny by the U.S. Congress*. Consequently, Wellcome and his exasperated wife travelled to Quito, Ecuador where the final tragic scenes of this prolonged marital drama were played out. Henry and Syrie were guests of Jordan Stabler of the American legation. The American diplomat's polo playing amigo's included the Ecuadorian dissident, Major J. S. Uribe and the American railroad magnate, Archer Harman. The proximity of these handsome, sporting, young men prompted Henry Wellcome to accuse Syrie of being unfaithful to him, perhaps in thought if not deed. However, Harman was cited as being the cause of the distress and Syrie vehemently denied any wrongdoing. Whether justified or not, the accusation succeeded in splintering any bond that the Wellcomes may have shared. The marriage, forged in the heat of the desert, had gradually dissipated in the mists of the Pyrenees, and then finally evaporated in the tropical heat of Central America. Syrie, indignantly, and perhaps, fearful of an uncertain future, retreated northward to New York City.

Above | Thomas John Barnardo photograph by Stepney Causeway Studio | For Better or Worse   111

Dr. Thomas John Barnardo and The Barnado Homes

Henry Wellcome's father in law was Dr. Thomas John Barnado who was born in Dublin on the 4th July 1845. Barnado arrived in London in 1866 with the intention of travelling to China as a missionary once he had trained as a doctor. What Barnado discovered in London would dramatically alter the course of his life, and the lives of thousands of children in Victorian London.

In 1866 London's east end suffered from poor housing, poverty and disease. The industrialisation of the city had a negative impact on the health of the population. Overcrowding compounded any outbreak of disease and 3,000 people had died in a cholera outbreak in the same year. As a result many orphaned children were sleeping on the streets and begging for help. When a young boy, Jim Jarvis, took Barnado to see numerous homeless children sleeping behind the parapet of a roof, Barnado decided to make the welfare of London's destitute children his life's work. He opened homes where the children could live safely, often learning a trade to sustain them as they grew older. When, in 1870, an 11 year old John Somers was found dead from malnutrition and exposure, having been previously turned away from the Stepney Causeway shelter, Barnado resolved that this would never happen again. Henceforth, the home bore the sign "No Destitute Child Ever Refused Admission". At the time of his death, in 1905, the charity ran 96 homes caring for 8,500 children. The charity Barnado's continues the work in the modern era.

Right Top | Group portrait of children outside a Barnardo home

Right Bottom | Dr. Barnardo's annual festival tea party given to destitute and homeless boys and girls, held at the Edinburgh Castle, Burdett Road, East London. About 1,000 boys and 150 girls attended. From: A newspaper 11th January, 1879

HOPE PLACE, WORLD'S END, E., WHERE DR. BARNARDO BEGAN HIS WORK

JIM JARVIS, HIS FIRST ARAB, SHOWING HIM A GROUP OF HOMELESS BOYS ASLEEP ON THE ROOF OF A HOUSE IN NOVEMBER 1866

DR. BARNARDO'S HOMES.

The "Raw Material" gathered in from the Slums of many Towns, and admitted on a single day!

1.—SERVING OUT THE TEA.   2.—SELECTING CANDIDATES FOR ADMISSION INTO THE HOMES.   3.—WAIFS FOR THE DOCTOR'S CARE.
4.—"TWO ORANGES AND TWOPENCE ON GOING OUT!"

DR: BARNARDO's FESTIVAL TO HOMELESS CHILDREN.

The Company Identity

"In the modern world of business, it is useless to be a creative original thinker unless you can also sell what you create. Management cannot be expected to recognise a good idea unless it is presented to them by a good salesman."

David M. Ogilvy

The Burroughs Wellcome partnership was formed in London in 1880, primarily as a sales agency promoting predominantly American pharmaceutical products in Europe. By October 1881, Silas Burroughs was embarking on a remarkably ambitious worldwide tour, establishing contacts and laying the foundations for a worldwide business. Burroughs tour covered the major developed population centres, both within and outside of the British Empire.

In London, the fledgling pharmaceutical business was struggling to stay afloat. The venture was lost in a sea of import duties, levied by the British government, and counterfeit products produced by rival companies in England. Wellcome's letters to Burroughs grudgingly acknowledged the clever imitations of the McKesson & Robbins products. This appreciation of the competition, however, did not prevent him from swiftly taking the necessary action to distance the company from its competitors. Initially this was done through various court actions brought to bear against unscrupulous rivals. Henry Wellcome, and his travelling business partner also recognised that the primary business model of marketing the imported compressed medicines of John Wyeth and McKesson Robbins needed urgent revision. At the helm of the business in London, Wellcome determined that the crisis could be overcome by establishing a manufacturing facility in England. The mass production of Burroughs Wellcome's own branded products, free of import duty, would maximise profits. The profits could then be reinvested into research and development of the range of drugs to supply the markets that Burroughs was developing worldwide. Through correspondence in the early 1880s, the partners agreed on the vital measures needed for both the protection and the expansion of their business.

On 25th March 1883 Wellcome signed a six year lease on a multi - property site at Bell Lane Wharf, Wandsworth. The South Bank Thameside site consisted of three separate units, and afforded the clean air and 50,000 gallons per day supply of fresh water that Wellcome deemed essential for the quality controlled production of pharmaceutical products. Within three months of acquiring the site, Henry Wellcome had installed and commissioned the plant and equipment to manufacture the full range of products previously purchased from external sources, including those previously imported from the U.S.A..

While Burroughs continued his epic, transcontinental, business expansion mission (he would not return to London until March 1884), Wellcome addressed the challenges of manufacturing, sales and distribution, marketing and advertising, as if he were cutting and polishing a valuable South African diamond. Every facet of business development was meticulously dealt with in turn by Wellcome and his trusted management team of Sudlow and Kirby.

The strategy of sending trained product salesmen to visit physicians and pharmacists was originally pioneered in England by Silas Burroughs. The scepticism of those diagnosing illness and prescribing remedies would only be convinced of the company's bona fide through the consistent quality of the products being recommended. The new relationship was further cemented by the establishment of the Physiological Laboratories in 1884. March of the same year also marked a major milestone, as the Tabloid name was registered exclusively for the branded products of the Burroughs Wellcome Company.

Manufacturing Chemists

The 6th of July 1889 saw the culmination of a decade of frantic business activity. The spectacular fireworks marking the opening of the Dartford works, may also have served as a reminder of the courtroom battle fought over company partnership issues earlier in the same year.

Ironically, the close collaboration required to provide an alternative facility to Wandsworth, was probably the finest hour of the partnership's first ten years.

The conversion of the former paper mills combined the talents of both Burroughs and Wellcome. The new site would provide the advanced research, manufacturing and enriched working conditions that the company aspired to.

A turning point in the company's fortunes had been reached. The explosion and fire which destroyed the Wandsworth works two months later would dramatically mark the end of an era.

Sales and Distribution

The carefully appointed offices in Snow Hill, Holborn, provided Burroughs Wellcome with a prestigious London headquarters for the international business. The addition of the quality controlled Dartford manufacturing plant, provided the confidence to meet the growing order books of the expanding sales force. Wellcome knew from his previous experience that manufacturing high quality products was only one ingredient of the recipe for success. The quality of the products would need to be preserved. Careful selection of the receptacles, stoppers, labelling, packing and shipping boxes would be required to ensure that the products reached their destination in prime condition. Repeated prescription and recommendation were required to sustain the future of the business. These important goals would only be achieved through consistency over many years. The means of transporting the products to market would evolve from one form of horsepower to another in the industrial age. Mass production methods of manufacture were required to keep the supply balanced with the demands of the consumer.

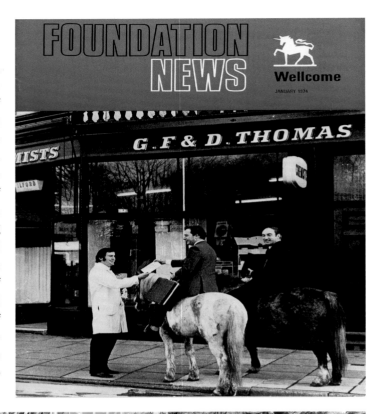

B. W. & Co. medical representatives and Head Office staff at the Carlisle B.M.A. Congress in 1896. Standing (left to right): Messrs. W. D. Howison, J. W. Rollings, G. E. Davis, W. E. Taylor, H. W. Lane, J. H. Harris, J. Dowdeswell, F. Ashley Rogers, Dr. Peter Short. Sitting: Messrs. Geo. E. Pearson, E. F. Linstead, W. R. Mealing, T. W. Davies, J. H. Francis, M. C. P. Irish, J. F. Burnett

Marketing and the British medical journals

The gaps in understanding and trust between patients, physicians and the pharmaceutical industry were initially bridged with the first publication of The Lancet in 1823. The weekly publication was the chief weapon used by Thomas Wakely in his campaign to expose, what he perceived to be, corruption and croneyism, in the medical profession. In October 2003, a project was announced to digitise every issue of the Lancet since its founding. The current editor, Richard Horton, remarked "Thomas Wakely and his successors have aimed to combine publication of the best medical science in the world with a zeal to counter the forces that undermine the value of medicine, be they political, social or cultural".

In the early 1880s, Henry Wellcome had the vision to realise that if his pharmaceutical business was going to endure, he would need to align himself and his company to the ethos of Wakely and his allies. Wellcome insisted that the marketing of Burroughs Wellcome products was designed exclusively for display in publications such as The Lancet, The British Medical Journal and The Chemist and Druggist. This policy would mean that the products would initially be subjected to the scrutiny of the medical profession, and in particular,

those with a keen eye for scientific research. When Frederick Belding Power joined the company as Chief Scientific Researcher in 1885, the company's credentials were further reinforced.

Below left | From the Chemist and Druggist Jan - March 1928. Burroughs Wellcome and Co. advertisement for Tabloid Photographic Chemicals

Below | The "Wellcome" exposure calculator in the back of the "Wellcome Photographic Exposure Record and Diary" 1914

Opposite page | 'Wellcome' Insulin, British Medical Journal

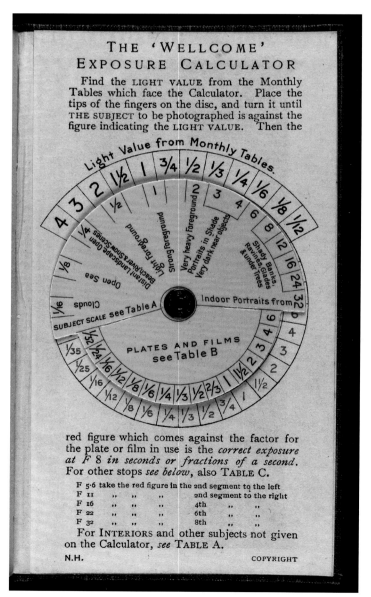

Reduced facsimile

PIONEERS AND EMPIRE BUILDERS: No. 576
NINTH PERIOD—circa A.D. 300 to c. 1300

Pure, Accurate and Reliable

TRADE MARK 'WELLCOME' BRAND INSULIN

Rubber-capped amber-glass phials of **100** *units in* **5** *c.c., at* **2/-** *each;* **200** *units in* **5** *c.c., at* **4/-** *each; and* **200** *units in* **10** *c.c., at* **4/-** *each*

Prices in London to the
Medical Profession

The Insulin Hydrochloride used in the preparation of 'Wellcome' Brand Insulin reaches a standard of purity approaching that of the purest Insulin ever obtained, even by research workers

'TABLOID' BRAND INSULIN HYDROCHLORIDE

No. 150—**2/-** *per carton containing* **10** *products in ONE tube*

No. 152—**2/8** *per carton of* **10** *tubes each containing ONE product*

Hypodermic   Sterile   10 UNITS

The only British Insulin issued as a compressed product

Accurate in dosage.   Solutions of any strength prepared instantly

BURROUGHS WELLCOME & CO., LONDON

Address for communications: SNOW HILL BUILDINGS. E.C.1

Exhibition Galleries: 10, Henrietta Street, Cavendish Square. W. 1

Associated Houses:
NEW YORK   MONTREAL   SYDNEY   CAPE TOWN   MILAN   BOMBAY   SHANGHAI   BUENOS AIRES

VIEW OF THE INTERIOR OF THE MOSQUE OF CORDOVA.— Buildings raised by or for the Arabians in the countries which they occupied were often modelled upon the local type, but modified to suit their needs or tastes. This resulted in originality. Moreover, the Arabians often took their materials from ancient structures on the spot, and the adaption of these alone led to important developments. Thus, columns found to be too short for the purpose were prolonged by placing vertical pieces between the capital and the spring of the arch, or even by superimposing a second column upon the capital; they masked these devices by making them the basis for skilful combinations of arcades.

DATE: A.D. c. 960   COPYRIGHT

Advertising the Cult of Beauty

Probably the most charming of the Burroughs Wellcome advertising campaigns was "The Cult of Beauty". This artistic and colourful group of posters extols the virtues of the Hazeline range. This product range was based on the natural ingredient of Witch Hazel, an astringent distilled from the bark and leaves of the North American Witch Hazel shrub. The plant was used medicinally by Native Americans. Hazeline skin products were one of the original beauty products marketed by Silas Burroughs in the early 1880s. The Hazeline trade mark was fiercely protected by Burroughs Wellcome, as the products were often imitated by rivals.

The car driving lady, in the fur collared coat, epitomises the profile of the emancipated heroine. Novels set in the 1920s, such as Evelyn Waugh's "Vile Bodies" and "Brideshead Revisited" describe the glamorous socialites of the age. Similarly, the dramatic poses struck by the models are reminiscent of early cinema posters. Wellcome's own sense of theatre and appreciation of the arts shines through the work.

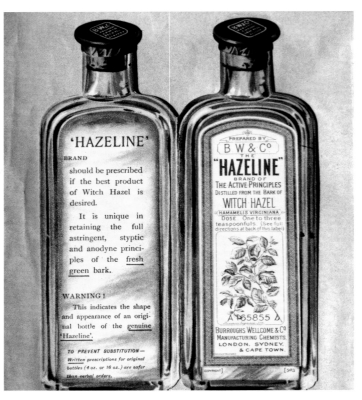

The Tabloid Evolution

Designed to refresh, revive and relax, the tabloid first aid kit was the first port of call for leisure sailors suffering a blow from a swinging boom. Burroughs Wellcome was the acceptable face of medicine in the early twentieth century. Presented in a user friendly format, emergency medicine was could now be self administered by the independent traveller. The carefully designed packaging surrounding the products was probably as reassuring to the accident prone recreational sailor, or unfortunate motorist, as the soothing products contained within. The neat personalised mass produced travel kits had, of course, evolved from the original larger custom designed kits supplied by Henry Wellcome to late 19th century explorers.

The tabloid concept had been borne out of the necessity to provide a more measured approach to the dispensing of medicinal products. Remarkably the concept of accurate dosing had not previously been dealt with. Medicinal cures could often be worse than the illness itself, inducing nausea and other symptoms in the patient. "It will either kill you or cure you" were words not too far from the truth prior to the careful measurement and compression of doses.

The concept of standardising dispensing proved to be a vital key to opening up foreign markets and duplicating the Burroughs Wellcome brand worldwide.

Below Left | 'Tabloid Medicine' Chest for Yachts in the shape of a life preserver c. 1920's

Below | Burroughs Wellcome and Company product: Tabloid Mixed Glands No. 2 tablets, Emprazil tablets and Tabloid Acetylsalicylic Aid tablets (Aspirin)

Right top | Tabloid First Aid Box showing contents - Quinine Sulphate blue bottle, Aromatic Ammonia tin and a selection of various tablets, thirst quenchers and sodas

Right bottom | 'Tabloid' Brand red first aid box

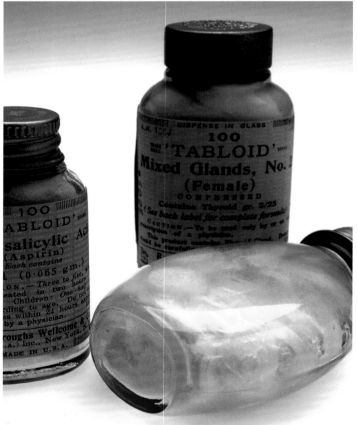

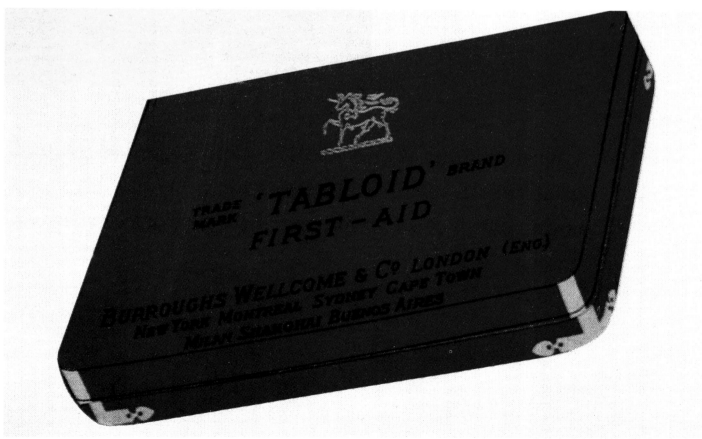

The Global Tabloid Revolution

Another significant step towards worldwide success in the pharmaceutical business came in March 1884 when Henry Wellcome registered the "Tabloid" brand as a patented trade mark of the Burroughs Wellcome Company. This date marked the breakthrough in the mass production of compressed medicines in the U.K. The future prospects of Burrroughs Wellcome would no longer be subject to the vagaries of American manufacturers, import duties and imitation.

The mass production machines designed to form the ovoid tablets were originally those of John Wyeth of Philadelphia, Silas Burroughs former employer. However, by 1887 Wellcome Burroughs improved tabloid manufacturing machines could compress tablets accurately at a rate of 600 per minute. Burroughs had specialised in compressed medicines at Philadelphia College, making it the subject of his 1877 graduation thesis.

The consumable products stamped out by these machines generated the profits that funded the global expansion of the Burroughs Wellcome Company.

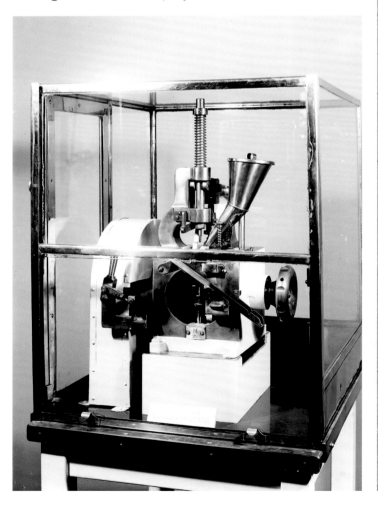

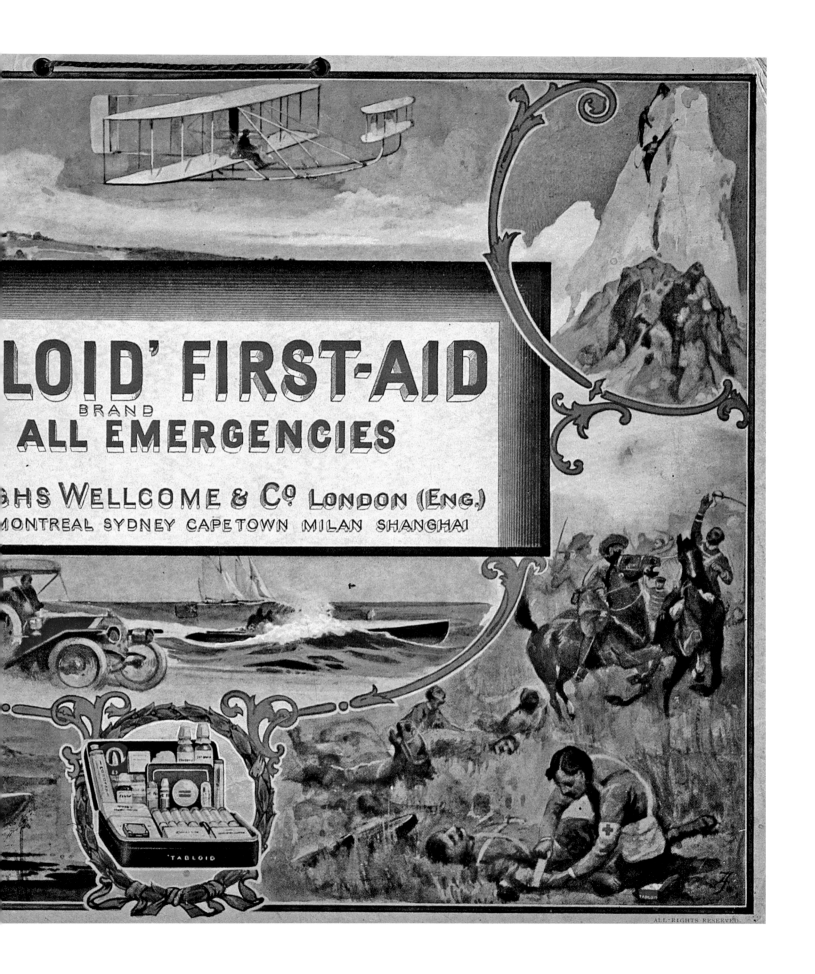

Above | Advertisemen showing various situations for the use of a Tabloid medicine chest | The Company Identity 127

BW&Co

PRODUCTS
STANDARDISE
DISPENSING
ALL OVER THE WORLD

No matter <u>when</u> or <u>where</u> the physician's prescriptions are dispensed — in the metropolis or in some country village; in any civilised land, or in some pioneer pharmacy on the fringe of the desert— the patient will receive medicaments of the same standard of activity, accuracy and dosage, <u>so long as the products of Burroughs Wellcome & Co. are specified.</u>

B. W. & Co. have offices and warehouses in every continent, and depots in every civilised community. Their products are stocked by, or are within the reach of, every pharmacist.

By prescribing B. W. & Co. products the physician safeguards his own reputation as well as his patient's welfare, and <u>simplifies dispensing for the foreign pharmacist.</u>

To ensure the supply of B. W. & Co. products the BRAND should always be written in full, thus— ℞ 'Tabloid'

BURROUGHS WELLCOME & CO., LONDON

NEW YORK   MONTREAL   SYDNEY   CAPE TOWN   MILAN   SHANGHAI   BUENOS AIRES

H 961 *Ex.*

Above | Another large containerised consignment of Wellcome products starts its journey | The Company Identity 129

Wartime Wellcome

In 1914 the outbreak of war in Europe must have brought to Henry Wellcome's troubled mind the words of his Uncle Silas, who, thirty-four years earlier had warned his nephew of the inevitability of a disastrous European conflict.

Henry Wellcome's response to the war was to immediately inform the War Office that all of his companies resources would be placed firmly behind the efforts of his adopted country. His old friend General Kitchener's call of "Your Country Needs You" was once again answered in full.

The research laboratories and the Dartford manufacturing works were expanded to meet the increased demand for vaccines against tetanus, gas gangrene and typhoid. Burroughs Wellcome also had to develop and manufacture great quantities of products only previously available from German manufacturers. These included Kharvisan, used to combat increased venereal disease during the war.

Wellcome also lobbied influential American's to support, the British war effort, in particular, Secretary of State Robert Lansing. Wellcome's pleas were politely declined as America would retain a neutral position on the calamitous European war until late in 1916.

Medicine and Surgery in the Great War 1914–1918

An Exhibition to commemorate the 50th anniversary of the Armistice, 11th November 1918
In the Museum of the Wellcome Institute of the History of Medicine
183 Euston Road London NW1

Open to the public 12th November 1968
Buses   14,18,30,73
Stations Euston, Euston Square, Warren Street

The Great Outdoors

Silas Burroughs and Henry Wellcome were both great exponents of the outdoor life. From Minnesota to Sudan, via Ecuador, expeditions, travel and exploration was a way of life for Henry Wellcome. With this lifestyle, Wellcome developed an appreciation of the needs of potential customers worldwide who would rely on Burroughs Wellcome products to help them cope with the great outdoors. Products were developed to deal with both apparent and hidden dangers, along with the minor irritants encountered in the countryside and outback from Aberdeen to Adelaide. These product ranges had evolved from the tabloid medical kits supplied to explorers and adventurers.

The diverse images employed in the adjacent advertising are remarkable examples of the artistic skills applied in pictorially illustrating a product's properties. The cartoon like drawings of the midge manic man, and particularly the allergy free picnickers are the stylistic, still image ancestors of 21st century television advertising campaigns. Lloyds Bank's 2010 storyboard of "the journey" of life, allied to the bank's products is particularly redolent of this delicate style of illustration from 1965. The family oriented feel compounds the similarities between the two.

Below left | The Age of Risks, 1914. Cover

Below | Advertisement for Burroughs Wellcome "Sketofax", insect repellent

Opposite page top | Advert for Histantin, a Burroughs Wellcome and Co. antihistamine agent. 1965

Opposite page bottom left | Instruction booklet for 'Tabloid' First Aid Snake Bite Kit 1943

Opposite page bottom right | Cover of "Tabloid fist aid for the mother "out back" from a booklet for the mothers of the Empire, who toiled bravely in the loneliness and solitudes of the Back o' Beyond

'Histantin'

Chlorcyclizine Hydrochloride (*Chlorcyclizine Tablets, B.P.*)

Authoritative opinion characterises 'HISTANTIN' as ". . . a very potent antihistaminic agent exhibiting a prolonged activity of twenty-four hours" (Jaros 1949) . . . which "does not sedate the patient, make him drowsy or incapacitate him from performing a full day's work." (Oliver 1952)

References

Jaros, S. H. (1949). *Ann. Allergy*, **7**, 466.
Oliver, R. (1952). *J. Irish med. Ass.*, **30**, 142.

Presentation

'Histantin' is issued as sugar-coated tablets, each of 50 mgm. (*Basic cost to N.H.S.: 4s. 1d. for 25 tablets*)
Also available for topical application:
'Histantin' brand Cream, in collapsible tubes of 17.5 gm. and jars of 1 lb. (*Basic cost to N.H.S.: 2s. 0d. for 17.5 gm. tube*)
'Histofax' brand Chlorcyclizine and Calamine Cream, in collapsible tubes of 17.5 gm. (*Basic cost to N.H.S.: 1s. 8d. plus P.T. for 17.5 gm. tube*)

 BURROUGHS WELLCOME & CO.
(*The Wellcome Foundation Ltd.*) LONDON

6798(H) · Printed in England   B.62.2.65

*"Il n'est que d'avoir
la clef des champs"*

The right food.

and how to

choose them

GENERAL RULES
WHEN PLANNIN

1. Eat all your ra
milk and cheese.

2. Eat a serving
vegetables daily
raw vegetable.

3. Fill up the cor
rationed energy f
one serving, or
potatoes every c

ISS

W.R.R. & Son Ltd. 1-3535

TO REMEMBER
YOUR DIET:

ns, not forgetting

correctly cooked
nd a serving of

rs with the un-
ds. Make sure of
referably two, of

BY THE MINISTRY OF FOOD

November, 1943.

Health and beauty *in war-time*

All Girls want to be healthy, fit and beautiful. Correct food plays a very important part in reaching this ideal.

How are you to know whether your meals are correctly planned or not? To answer this question you should know the part food plays in the working of the body.

All the different kinds of foods can be placed in one of three groups :

  I. Fuel or energy foods
  II. Body building and repairing foods.
  III. Protective foods.

Some foods, such as milk and potatoes, go into more than one group.

The foods which belong to each group, and their uses to the body, are explained in this folder

There's a Time for Work and a Time for Play

"Shared laughter creates a bond of friendships. When people laugh together, they cease to be young and old, teacher and pupils, worker and boss. They become a single group of human beings."

W. Lee Grant

The Victorian era spawned many forms of philanthropy. As the population shifted from rural areas to industrialising cities, the weak and vulnerable would often fall deeper into poverty. Poor standards of housing, a lack of sanitation and chronic overcrowding were endemic. When disease struck the weakest constitutions, a downward spiral would often ensue. As a result, the life expectancy of a working class Londoner in the 1840s could be well below thirty years.

As the century progressed, the inability of the State to deal with the needs of its people created a void which charitable organisations and concerned individuals would attempt to fill. A difference of opinion emerged between those with the means to make a difference. For example, the mission of Dr. J. T. Barnado would pride itself on never refusing admission to a destitute child, however, the Charitable Organisation Society led by C. S. Loch regarded efforts such as Barnado's as counterproductive. Loch argued that an indiscriminate response to the immediate needs of the poor would foster a culture of dependency. This philosophy was derived, in part, from a book written in 1859 by Samuel Smiles, entitled simply, "Self Help". Limited resources would often be targeted at the 'deserving poor', for example, those who would abstain from drink and follow a path of righteous living. Housing reformer, Octavia Hill, pioneered case social work, with families removed from slum dwelling into improved housing. The tenancy was conditional upon the carefully selected tenant's ability to maintain certain monitored standards of housekeeping and behaviour.

Victorian England's disparate benevolent societies and individuals, remarkably, seemed able to reach a consensus on an arguably controversial policy. In an effort to reduce the number of mouths to feed, many thousands of hapless individuals, who were unable to be supported through hard times, were transported to the various colonies of the British Empire. The one-way passages to Canada and Australia were paid for by the philanthropists in an effort to both relieve the desperate situation at home, and populate the colonies abroad.

A tradition of corporate social responsibility also emerged in the Victorian age. The main concern for working families was that of finding adequate housing. The wealthy industrialists began to address this situation by constructing 'model villages' for their employees. By developing these early live-work communities, industrialists such as Sir Titus Salt would greatly improve the lot of their employees. Saltaire's terraced rows were connected to mains drainage and solidly built from local stone by the artisans of Bradford. Parkland promenades were incorporated into the scheme, public houses were not. The fortunate employees were encouraged to eschew the 'demon drink'. George and Richard Cadbury built the garden community of Bournville to serve the needs of their confectionery workers. Similarly, the Quaker, Joseph Rowntree founded New Earswick near York.

Silas Burroughs and Henry Wellcome may not have been singing from the same hymn sheet, however, the initiative to relocate the company's research and manufacturing facilities into the Kent countryside was a truly inspired one in terms of employee welfare. The motto "A time for work and a time for play" defined the considered design of the available space.

VICTORIAN GUARDIANS OF THE WORKS

This classical photograph of the Wellcome Chemical Works Fire Brigade was taken in approximately 1898. Back row (left to right) : Third Officer Bargate and Firemen Purnett, Sloss, Spencer, Shackleton, Thomas, Taylor, Casey and Lepper. Middle row : Firemen Purton, Stacey and Dartnell, Second Officer Alderton, Fireman Neighbour, name not known, and Fireman Smith. Front row : Firemen Hardy and Ney, Chief Officer Morris, and Firemen Herbert and Brooker. Sons and daughters of some of these include Mr. W. Neighbour, compressing engineer with 43 years' service, Mr. C. W. Dartnell, shop foreman in the Engineers with 40 years' service, whose father gave this photograph some years ago to Captain Peters, and Miss J. Herbert (now Mrs. Fenner), of the Forwarding Department

7

Above | Maypole Dance at the 25th Anniversary Fete, 15th July, 1905, in the grounds of the Wellcome Club and Institute, Dartford, Kent

INTERIOR OF GYMNASIUM AND ASSEMBLY ROOM

Above | Interior of gymnasium and assembly hall. From: The Evolution of Journalism. Burroughs Wellcome 1909
Below | Packing girls in the Dartford site dining room

...a Time for Play

With the rejuvenated lake sparkling like the 'jewel in the crown', the Dartford works garden site was idyllic. Silas Burrough's tragically premature death in 1895 predated the opening of Acacia Hall in 1899. The Hall's substantial grounds were animated by all manner of physical activity, including football, cricket, tennis, boating and swimming. The vigorous Mr. Burroughs, would have undoubtedly approved of these life enhancing developments in employee welfare. Ironically, an ill advised bicycle ride on the Cote' d 'Azur, during a period of convalescence, had contributed to his own unfortunate demise. The Wellcome Club and Institute contained a clubhouse, gymnasium and a library. Wellcome gave books as presents to his staff every Christmas. Literary and music societies were encouraged alongside concerts and staff outings. The prescribed eight hour working day left plenty of leisure time to enjoy the impressive amenities. Employment prospects for Dartford's population were rising again with the rebirth of the Phoenix mills site. Employee numbers rose from 349 in 1897 to 769 by April 1899.

Frontiers of Science

"Every scientific fulfillment raises new questions; it asks to be surpassed and outdated."

Max Weber

Henry Wellcome's fascination with scientific research was born out of his affinity with the natural world. From an early age, the interdependency between human beings, animals and plant life was very apparent to Wellcome. The awareness was sharpened by his boyhood experiences, including an overland trek from the blighted, barren, Wisconsin prairies to the fertile fields, and fast flowing waters of the Minnesota valley. His empathy with the native American population further enhanced his keen observers eye for nature's own remedies, and aids to survival.

It seems fitting that a vaccine for diphtheria was developed from equine sources, by a man who was dependent upon a mule for transport through the treacherous Peruvian and Ecuadorian landscape. It is not a coincidence that Wellcome's South American expedition was undertaken in the pursuit of naturally derived sustainable products.

One of Wellcome's finest talents was that of recognising the talents of others working around him. As a student in Chicago and Philadelphia, it became apparent to him that his good friend, Frederick Belding Power, was uniquely gifted as a scientific researcher. Wellcome's own attributes, would, in time, enable him to direct his business towards a more innovative path. The physiological research facilities established in Dartford had initially been used for sample testing and quality control of the various manufacturing processes. The appointment of Fred Power in 1895 heralded Wellcome's commitment to the scientific research required to develop new drug therapies. This strategy would prove vital to the longevity of the company.

At the turn of the century, Henry Wellcome's journeys in and out of North Africa, were allied to the cause of ridding Khartoum of insect borne disease. In establishing the Wellcome Tropical Research Laboratory, under Andrew Balfour's energetic stewardship, Wellcome, Balfour and Charles Morley Wenyon developed the fundamental principles of hygiene required in the fight for human survival. The methods devised in making Khartoum inhabitable would later be transferred to other blighted areas of the planet including the Panama Canal Zone in Central America.

Risk and reward were the realities balanced by both American and European entrepreneurs in the second half of the 19th century. In this respect, Alfred Nobel and Henry Wellcome were kindred spirits. Both were driven by the quest to reveal the secrets held thus far by Mother Nature. In Nobel's case, his father's influence as the inventor of the shipping mine during the Crimean war, would eventually lead him to discover that a carefully measured cocktail of Nitric and Sulphuric acid, mixed with glycerine, would produce an unpredictably explosive compound. Nobel's time would subsequently be dedicated to harnessing the destructive and constructive power of nitroglycerine. The end product, dynamite, would enable civil engineering projects that were previously thought to be beyond the power of mankind. The Panama Canal being the most prominent example.

Right | A mosquito in flight with its abdomen full of blood. Through its role in the transmission of malaria and yellow fever, it is claimed that the mosquito has killed more than half the humans that have ever lived and it continues to kill between one and two million people a year, mainly young children. Anopheles Stephensi, (pictured) is the insect vector that transmits malaria in India and Pakistan.

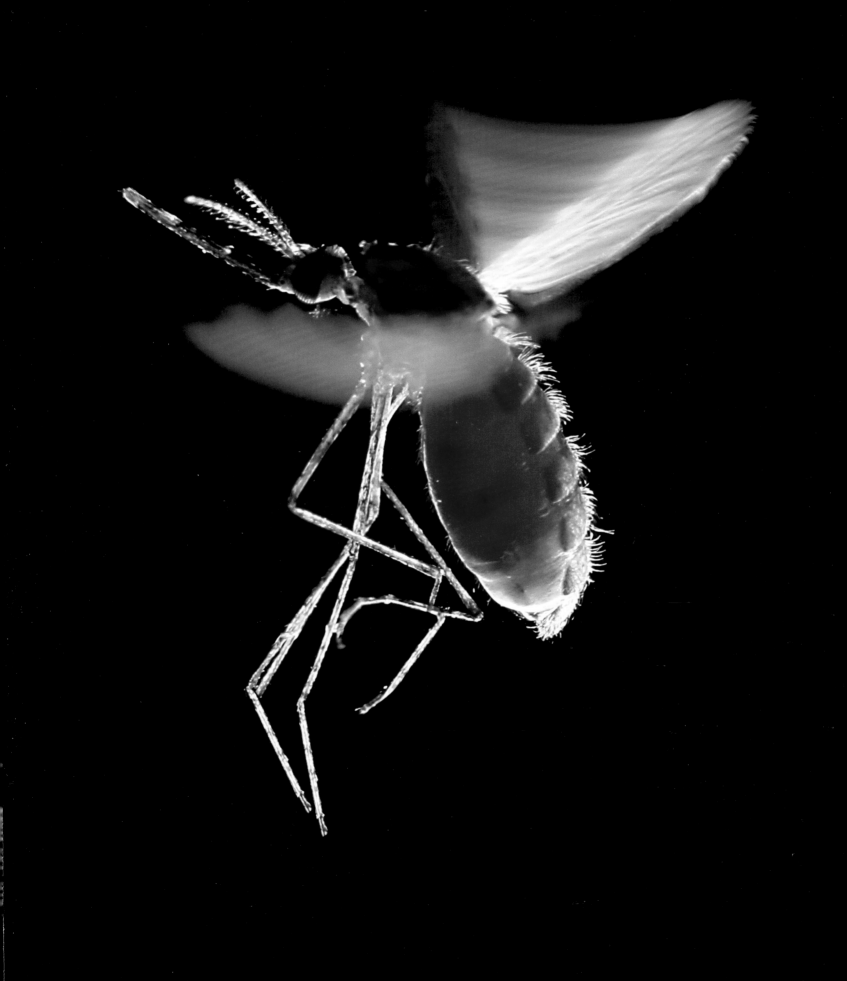

The Nobel Prize in Physiology or Medicine, 1936

Alfred Nobel died in his home in San Remo, Italy on 10th December 1896. Nobel's last will required the establishment of the Nobel Prize for outstanding achievements in physics, chemistry, physiology or medicine, literature and for work in peace. The first prizes were awarded in 1901.

On the 29th October 1936, only three months after the death of Sir Henry Wellcome, the Nobel Prize for Physiology or Medicine was awarded to Sir Henry Hallet Dale and Proffessor Otto Loewi. The prize was awarded for Dale and Loewi's work in "revealing the mode through which impulses communicate their signal across the miniscule gaps, or synapses, that separate nerve cells from each other and from their target destinations".

Wellcome's will, read to Dale that same year, requires the Wellcome Trust to provide funds for "the advancement of medical and scientific research to improve mankind's wellbeing". The discernible difference between the two organisations is that the Nobel Institute awards prizes and the Wellcome Trust is likely to fund the work that wins them.

Both Alfred Nobel and Sir Henry Wellcome had the vision to leave a legacy designed to inspire future generations.

Below left | Sir Henry Dale and King Gustav V of Sweden

Below | Left side of Nobel Prize awarded to Sir Henry Dale and Prof. Otto Loewi in 1936

Opposite Top | The King of Sweden presents Nobel prizes in Stockholm to Prof. Otto Loewi, Sir Henry Dale, Prof. Peter Debye, Dr. C. D. Anderson, Prof. Hess

Opposite Bottom Left | Right side of Nobel Prize awarded to Sir Henry Dale and Prof. Otto Loewi in 1936

Opposite Bottom Right | Sir Michael Perrin, Sir Henry Hallett Dale and King Gustav V of Sweden

Pioneering Rational Drug Design

1966 to 1986 were the golden years in Wellcome's world of scientific research. At the centre of the most valuable drug discoveries were George Hitchins and Gertrude Elion who worked together at the Burroughs Wellcome Research Laboratories in New York, and subsequently, North Carolina. The key to the scientist's success was their pioneering method of investigating specific molecular targets for potential drugs as opposed to a trial and error approach. The new method became known as rational drug design.

The first effective leukemia drug, 6-mercapopurine (6-MP) was developed in this way. The same method then allowed Hitchins and Elion to develop a number of drugs related to 6-MP which suppressed the immune system. These drugs would allow patients to receive organ transplants without their bodies rejecting the new organs.

In developing Allopurinol, the team were able to effectively treat gout by reducing the body's production of uric acid which can build up in the joints of the human body.

Gertrude Elion's research was also vital in the development of Acyclovar. This anti-viral drug causes interference in the replication process of the herpes virus. The AIDS medication, AZT, was derived by Elion's colleagues following the same principles.

In 1988, George Hitchins (1905 - 1998) and Gertrude Elion (1918 - 1999) were jointly awarded the Nobel Prize in Physiology or Medicine, together with James Whyte Black.

Below | Nobel prize winners Dr. Hitchings and Dr. Elion

Opposite Top Left | Amoxycillin capsules

Opposite Top Right | Wellcome Polio vaccine administered on a sugar lump c. 1980

Opposite Bottom | Retrovir, an anti-retroviral drug, the first approved for treatment of HIV c. 1995

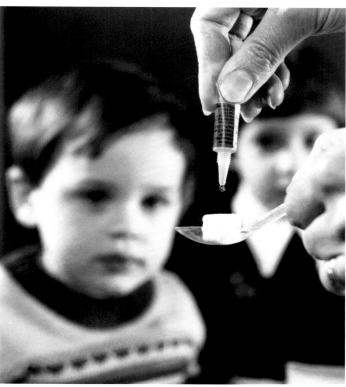

DNA

Right | Stem cell research: researcher picking colonies of cultured human stem cells 2006

Below | Inside DNA: A Genomic Revolution is a unique Wellcome Trust funded exhibition at the Explore-At-Bristol Centre. It investigates developments in the fast-moving field of human genomics, and the ethical issues that they raise.

Inside DNA encourages visitors to explore issues such as the role of our genes and environment in our health, identity and evolution. It delves into ethical questions such as whether genetic testing will lead to discrimination, who will benefit most from genetic medicines, and the role of DNA databases. This was funded with a Capital Award.
Photograph 19/12/2007

Opposite Page | Crick's sketch of genetic code 13 April 1965. Gordon Research Conference 1965 - 66

2nd

1st ↓	U	C	A	G	3rd ↓
U	PHE	SER	TYR	CYS	U
	PHE	SER	TYR	CYS	C
	LEU	SER	Ochre c.T.	?	A
	LEU	SER	Amber c.T.	Tryp	G
C	((leu)) LEU	PRO	HIS	ARG	U
	Leu	PRO	His	ARG	C
	leu,	PRO	GLUN	ARG	A
	(leu)	PRO	GLUN	ARG	G
A	ILEU	THR	ASPN	(ser) SER	U
	ILEU	THR	ASPN	((ser))	C
	? ~~xxxx~~ ILEU	THR	LYS	((arg)) ARG	A
	MET	THR	LYS	(arg)	G
G	VAL	ALA	ASP	GLY	U
	VAL	ALA	ASP	GLY	C
	VAL	(Ala) ALA	GLU	(Gly)	A
	Val	ALA	Glu		G

Capitals = Nirenberg's results

others = other ~~xxxxx~~ results and other sources.

13th April '65

Flee.

Wellcome's Legacy and The Work of the Trust

"With the enormous possibility of development in chemistry, bacteriology, pharmacy and allied sciences... there are likely to be vast fields opened for productive enterprise for centuries to come."

Sir Henry S. Wellcome

1936 - 1945

Henry Wellcome died peacefully at the London Clinic on 25th July, 1936 and was cremated at Golders Green Cemetery. When Peter Williams moved into the office of the Director of the Wellcome Museum he found the urn containing Sir Henry's ashes residing in the bookcase. Dr. Williams considered that "a more appropriate place" should be found. Consequently, arrangements were made and, in 1987 Sir Henry's ashes were buried in the churchyard of St. Paul's Cathedral and a plaque placed on the wall of the crypt.

Sir Henry Wellcome's will, which he signed in 1932, established the Wellcome Trust. The will stated that the entire share capital of the Wellcome Foundation Ltd should be held by five Trustees who would be responsible for spending the income to advance medical research and the understanding of its history.

The Wellcome Foundation Ltd was a limited liability company established by Sir Henry in 1924. This company encompassed the worldwide pharmaceutical business, the research laboratories and Sir Henry's entire collection. All the shares in this company were wholly owned by Sir Henry. The first board of five Trustees was formed in 1936 and consisted of Henry Dale and Thomas Renton Elliott who were both scientists, G. H. H. Lyall (Chairman) and Claude Bullock (both lawyers} the fifth man was accountant Martin Price.

G. H. H. Lyall died in 1937 and was succeeded by Sir Henry Dale who became the Chairman in 1938. Dale was one of Britain's most eminent scientists, having won the Nobel Prize in 1936 for his work on neuro-humoral transmission. Sir Henry Dale was to remain as Chairman until 1960.

Above | Portrait of G. H. H. Lyall, the first Chairman of the Wellcome Trust

Opposite top | The last portrait taken of Sir Henry Wellcome

Opposite bottom | Pocket watch found in Sir Henry's pocket at the time of his death, 12.40 am., 25 July 1936.
An engraving on the watch reads, 'Presented to William John White by BW and Co for 21 years service 7 November 1900'

The number of Trustees was temporarily reduced to four until J. E. K. (Jack) Clarke joined the Board as Secretary to the Trustees.

The only science grant awarded in 1938, prolonged the work of Dr. Foy at the Tropical Research Unit in Thessaloniki, Greece. This malarial research unit was taken over by the Wellcome Trust following an appeal for funding by the League of Nations.

The great challenge for the Trustees was to administer the will of Sir Henry Wellcome, with regard to the vast, eclectic collection and the satisfactory closure and documentation of the excavations in the Sudan and Palestine. The excavations were successfully closed by the advent of World War II, however, the task of assessing the archaeological digs and the retrieved artifacts would only be concluded by the eventual publication of the Lachish Letters in 1938 and the main archaeological report by Frank Addison on Jebel Moya published in 1955

The bombing of Snow Hill in 1941 further exacerbated the problem of cataloguing the extensive unpacked collection stored at Euston Road as space, originally designated for Museum display became urgently required as business premises.

THE WELLCOME ARCHAEOLOGICAL RESEARCH EXPEDITION TO THE NEAR EAST

LACHISH I
(TELL ED DUWEIR)

THE LACHISH LETTERS
BY
HARRY TORCZYNER
BIALIK PROFESSOR OF HEBREW IN THE UNIVERSITY OF JERUSALEM

LANKESTER HARDING

ALKIN LEWIS

J. L. STARKEY

PUBLISHED FOR
THE TRUSTEES OF THE LATE SIR HENRY WELLCOME
BY THE
OXFORD UNIVERSITY PRESS
LONDON   NEW YORK   TORONTO
1938

Above | Interior of Snow Hill Buildings in 1885 which was the headquarters of the Wellcome firm from 1884 - 1939. Designed by Henry Wellcome.

Above | Exterior of Burroughs Wellcome and Co.'s head offices, Snow Hill c. 1885
Below | Carved panelling interior to the North East corner

Above | In 1941 the Snow Hill headquarters was destroyed by a German bombing raid |

1946 - 1955

Sir Henry Dale remained as Chairman throughout this post-war period. Sir Henry Wellcome's enterprises and affairs had been many and complex. The Trust was instrumental in selling and donating collection items not directly related to the history of medicine, although the collections, museums and library were still owned by the Foundation. During this time, the assets of the Trust were reduced as a result of paying high duties on Sir Henry's estate.

In 1953, the Wellcome Centenary Exhibition at Euston Road celebrated 100 years since the birth of Sir Henry Wellcome on August 21st, 1853. The exhibition was opened on the 8th July by Winthrop W. Aldrich, the American Ambassador to London. Designed by the Wellcome Historical Medical Museum, the displays reflected Sir Henry Wellcome's lifetime of collecting, comprising artifacts from the United States through to the archaeological finds from the Sudan and Palestine. Other features of the exhibition included contributions from Wellcome's numerous research laboratories. The exhibition was reported in the July 4th edition of the journal, Nature.

In 1953, Michael Perrin succeeded Mr H. E. Sier as Chairman of the Wellcome Foundation Ltd.. Perrin persuaded the Trust to invest the Foundation's profits into the research and development of new drugs. This initiative would eventually result in the production of drugs developed under the guidance of George Hitchins and Trudy Elion at the Burroughs Wellcome laboratories in the USA. In bringing these drugs to the market, the Foundation's profits increased and a precedent was set for the creation of wealth and the future prosperity of the Trust.

In 1955, the Burroughs Wellcome Fund was established by Sir Henry Dale and William N. Creasy, president and chair of Burroughs Wellcome Co., USA. The vision was for the Burroughs Wellcome Fund to be a United States extension of the Wellcome Trust.

The Trustees remained faithful to Sir Henry Wellcome's will. Thirty-five per cent of the funds were allocated to tropical and veterinary medicine, pharmacy and pharmacology and the history of medicine. The remaining sixty-five per cent was spent on the provision of laboratories, libraries and museums. This financial support was aimed specifically at scientists in universities rather than those in industry.

The global reach of the Company was demonstrated in the form of travel grants and fellowships for UK scientists travelling abroad and in enabling overseas researchers to visit the UK. The Trust report for the first 20 years declared a charitable expenditure of £1.2 million.

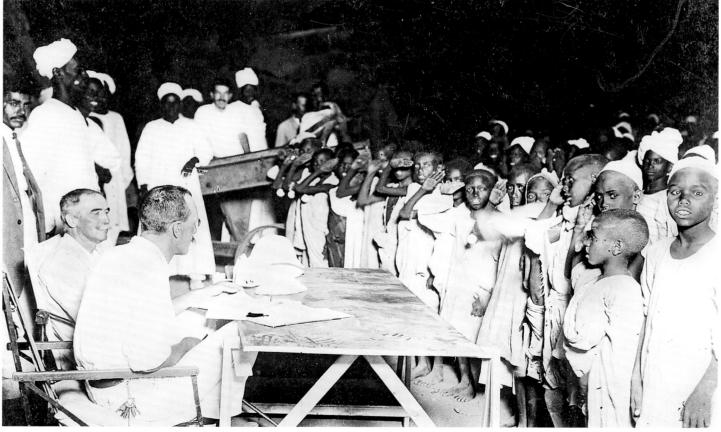

Above | Sir Henry Wellcome, staff and boys, Wellcome excavations, Jebel Moya, Sudan

THE WELLCOME EXCAVATIONS IN THE SUDAN

Above | Artefacts from Jebel Moya displayed at The Wellcome Centenary Exhibition 1953 | Wellcome's Legacy 161

1956 - 1965

Sir Henry Dale continued as Chairman until 1960 when he became Chief Scientific Advisor. He was to continue in this role until 1966.

Lord William Piercy was appointed to succeed Dale as Chairman in 1960, Lord Piercy died in 1966. Lord Franks was appointed as the Chairman of the Trust in 1965.

The Trust's fortunes steadily rose throughout this period as a result of being sole share holder of the Wellcome Foundation. These results were reflected in the £8.5 million awarded to support biomedical research and the history of medicine. Sixty per cent of this total was allocated to research laboratories and equipment.

By 1966 a total of 83 Trust funded buildings had been constructed worldwide, including the Wellcome Institute for Research, Nairobi, Kenya. In the state of Tamil Nadu in South India, the Sprue Research Unit was funded by the Wellcome Trust and in Jamaica an epidemiological research unit was built. This demonstrated the Trust's policy of not competing with State funded projects. The Medical Research Council Laboratories in Gambia were presented with The Lady Dale river boat to aid their field work. The largest grant awarded in the U.S.A. was £90,000 to supplement the cost of extending the Pharmacology

Laboratories at Yale University School of Medicine. This project facilitated Yale becoming one of the most active pharmacology departments in the world, specializing in anti-cancer agents.

Gradually, the focus of the Trust's funding was to change towards that of career support via short term project grants. This policy was reinforced through the creation of senior fellowships for clinicians taking up academic research. Furthermore, the fund was instrumental in University College, London establishing the first history of medicine department in the UK.

The Trust continued to struggle with the complexity of Sir Henry Wellcome's vast collections. In a further effort to reduce their size, the prehistoric collections were donated to the British Museum in 1965. The Egyptology collections were also dispersed, with some 90 cases received by Liverpool Museum. In 1966, the Ethnographic Collection was donated to the University of California, Los Angeles, USA.. The majority of the exhibits consisted of Native American artifacts collected in the 1920s by anthropologists hired by Sir Henry.

Towards the end of this period the Trust began to establish important investment powers for the future, with a view to increasing funds independent of its shareholding in the Wellcome Foundation.

1966 - 1985

With the 1960s in full swing the Wellcome Foundation's profitability continued to grow, resulting in the Wellcome Trust spending totalling £26.1 million through the ten years from 1966. This was triple the expenditure of the previous ten years. Forty-four per cent of the funding was directed towards supporting careers and research expenses, particularly in the fields of tropical medicine in collaboration with the World Health Organisation. The trustees increased their number from five to seven and appointed Peter Williams as the first Director of the Trust. To ensure that the increased spending was used judiciously, expert advisory panels were formed to scrutinise the key areas of global funding. Previously neglected fields such as dermatology and mental health were targeted by offering grants and training fellowships to attract researchers into these subjects. Another significant initiative was the Trust's endeavour to reverse the trend of talented scientific researchers moving from Britain and Europe to the U.S.A.. In an effort to reverse the "brain drain" an innovative University Awards scheme absorbed thirty-five per cent of all spending. Furthermore, the Trust collaborated with other European charitable bodies in recognising the need to engage in Science Policy. In London, the historical medical collections were loaned to The Science Museum in an effort to fund the Wellcome Library facility at Euston Road.

Grant allocations for 1976 - 1986 of £169 million were made possible by sales in excess of £1billion per annum, largely due to the success of the anti-viral drugs acyclovir and AZT. Sir David Steel became Chairman of the Trustees in 1982 and was influential in increasing the Trust's income through the sale of shares on the stock market. As result the Trust's holdings in the newly formed Wellcome plc reduced from 100 to 75 per cent. Income from the flotation was diversely reinvested by the Trust.

Career awards were developed for academic researchers in basic and clinical medicine encouraging senior lectureships and targeted training fellowships in toxicology, ophthalmology and mental health.

Facility support during this period was mainly focused on UK laboratories, and overseas, research units in India, Jamaica, Kenya and Thailand also benefitted. Furthermore, in a move to improve tropical medicine. The Trust joined forces with the WHO and Rockerfeller Foundation.

Above | Oliver Sherwill Franks, Baron Franks of Headington. By Robert N. Hepple R.A. 1990 | Wellcome's Legacy 165

1986 - 1995

In 1986 the Trust celebrated its 50th birthday. A soiree held at the Wellcome Building was attended by Her Majesty the Queen and the Duke of Edinburgh.

Throughout this period the policy of reducing the Trust's shareholding in Wellcome plc resulted in Glaxo plc eventually becoming the majority shareholder resulting in the creation of Glaxo Wellcome plc.

The Trust created a new constitution and a new company 'The Wellcome Trust Ltd'. This was a private limited company, the Trustees become Governors and were responsible for its expenditure and investments. As a result, the Trust made larger and more long term commitments, more programme grants were funded and its first multimillion pound awards were allocated.

The newly refurbished Wellcome Building at 183 Euston Road became the new Trust Headquarters, housing administrative staff, the Wellcome Institute for the History of Medicine and a new Wellcome Centre for Medical Science.

A positive move was the development of the Trust's career awards structure which was devised to support clinical and basic science researchers from students and training fellowships to high level Principal Research Fellowships and

was instrumental in improving academic research salaries. Investments include The PRISM (Policy Research in Science and Medicine) unit which was created to improve procedures to assess the outcome of the Trust's investment in research, and to provide factual information for the wider community to help it argue the case for medical research funding. PRISM was believed to be the first group anywhere in Europe to be primarily concerned with medical research policy.

Another development was the Sanger Centre (later renamed the Wellcome Trust Sanger Institute) which was established by the Trust and the Medical Research Council as an advanced facility for mapping, sequencing and decoding the human genome and the genomes of other organisms. The Trust committed an initial £44 million to the project.

Sir Roger Gibbs became Chairman of the Trust in 1989,

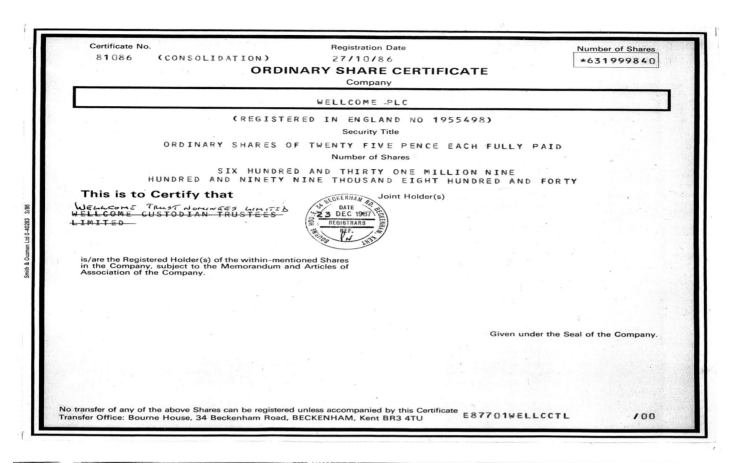

Above | Representation of Anglo-American research on the human genome. B. Sanderson 1990 | Wellcome's Legacy   167

The Sanger Institute, a key player in the international Human Genome Project, was responsible for sequencing one-third of the genome, a first draft of which was announced in 2000. This centre also became the focus of programmes in pathogen sequencing, functional and structural genomics and the HapMap Consortium, cataloguing human genetic variation. By 2006 this accounted for 15 per cent of the Trust's expenditure. Tropical medical research funding support abroad was increased by the Trust, especially in malaria. Major programmes in South-east Asia and Africa were financed.The Trust also co-funded the National Science Learning Centre at York, providing access to teaching resources and expertise in contemporary science, this helped to shape the new GSCE science syllabus 'Twenty First Century Science'. At the turn of the century the Trust was the largest non-governmental funder of millennium projects providing over £33m to science centres and museums.

Right | The output from an automated DNA sequencing machine used by the Human Genome Project to determine the complete human DNA sequence.

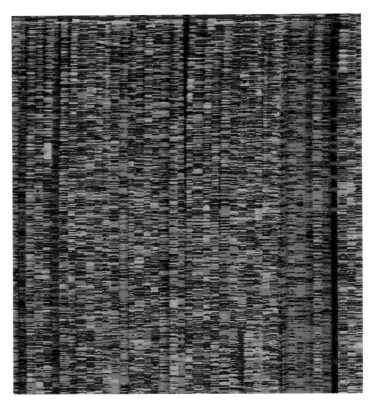

2006 and into the future

The annual research expenditure increased from an average of £28 million in the 1980s to £650 million in 2007.

The Trust has transformed its investment policy and combined aligned partnerships with the strongest external managers, building in-house resources to own selected assets directly. The internal investment team has been strengthened establishing a more robust approach for managing investment risk. The Board of Governors determines the broad structure of the Trust's asset management arrangements. Responsibility for implementation is delegated to the Investment Committee and the Investment team.

The Trust also became the only UK-domiciled non-public-sector organisation to gain a AAA credit rating, and the first UK charity to issue a listed bond.

The Wellcome Trust recently published a Strategic Plan 2010–20 which describes the Trust's vision and mission statement as follows:

"Our vision is to achieve extraordinary improvements in human and animal health" and that "Our mission is to support the brightest minds in biomedical research and the medical humanities."

In the foreword, The Chairman, Sir William Castell, who was appointed in 2007, describes the way forward in the next decade : "This Plan for the next decade provides the basis on which we will develop our funding strategies. It sets out how we will assess progress towards our goals, so that we can help to realise extraordinary improvements in health". The Trust focus for funding is stated in the Strategic Plan as:

1. Supporting outstanding researchers by supporting the brightest and best researchers, seizing emerging strategic opportunities, building world-class research environments and influencing the policy and funding landscape.

2. Accelerating the application of research by accelerating product development, supporting clinical translation and stimulating uptake of research to policy and practice.

3. Exploring medicine in historical and cultural contexts by placing medicine within a cultural context, inspiring and educating young people, embedding mutual trust and understanding and opening up information.

...Knighthood

"Life would be infinitely happier if we could only be born at the age of eighty and gradually approach eighteen"

Mark Twain

Henry Solomon Wellcome, became Sir Henry Solomon Wellcome, Knight of the British Empire, when the New Year's Honours were announced in the London Chronicle in January 1932. The honour, was by decree of His Majesty King George V. It seems unlikely that as a boy in Minnesota, Henry Wellcome would ever have dreamed of such an honour, as he diligently began his lifelong education in the log cabin school in Garden City. As Sir Henry came towards the end of his life's journey, the honour bestowed upon him by the reigning monarch of his adopted country was long overdue. Sir Henry's contribution to the health and well being of the British Empire, its soldier's and its subjects had been evident since the turn of the century in Sudan and WWI.

The dedication to Sir Henry's chosen field of work had already resulted in him being awarded a Life Membership of the American Pharmaceutical Society. Having also been granted the Freedom of the Society of Apothecaries of the City of London in January 1931, Sir Henry had been honoured on both sides of the Atlantic. However, perhaps the honour that filled him with the most circumspect pride, was not the Knighthood, but the one bestowed upon him by the Royal College of Surgeons in March 1932, when Sir Henry became an Honorary Fellow. His thoughts on that day may well have taken him back seventy years, across 3,000 miles of ocean and a further 2,500 miles of the Western American landscape. Back to the dangerous boyhood days endured during the Sioux uprising, when he bravely assisted his Uncle, Dr. J. W. B. Wellcome, in tending the wounds of the injured settlers of Minnesota.

Sir Henry may also have felt some satisfaction that the dedication to his professional life had at long last been publicly rewarded. Since the premature death of his business partner, Silas Burroughs, and the tragic collapse of his marriage, Sir Henry's life had been of a solitary nature, devoid of the j'oie de vivre evident in his pre-marital years in the London of the 1890s. Having earned the respect and admiration of his peers, he was now able to celebrate his achievements with his fellows in medicine, towards the end of a life spent furthering its causes.

An optimistic outlook on life and an exuberant sense of fun characterised the young Henry Wellcomes early life. As a boy, Henry was chastised for his practical jokes by a father who preached restraint and moderation as a way of life. Sir Henry's lifelong adventure may well have started as a personal rebellion and undoubtably saddened by the personal tragedy of his marriage to, and divorce from, Syrie Barnado, ended immersed in the conventions of academic and civic society. The sense of duty instilled by Wellcome's parents may well have won through in the end.

When disease finally assaulted one of its greatest adversaries, Sir Henry could have accepted his fate knowing that he had fought the good fight, and in doing so inspired subsequent generations to continue his work. The Wellcome name is now synonymous with the advancement of medical science and the wellbeing of mankind. On a human level, it is also evident that Sir Henry also immensely enjoyed his life and the great opportunities afforded him by his endeavours.

Right | Sir Henry Wellcome. Bronze bust by G. F. Edgardo Simone 1930

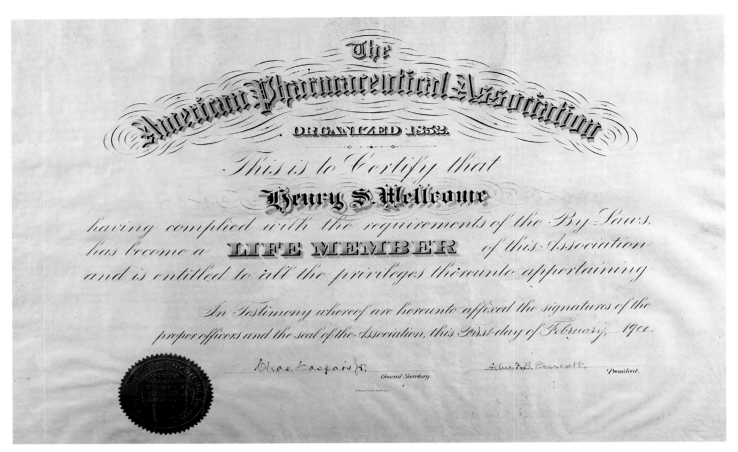

Royal College of Surgeons of England.

Know all Men by these Presents that

We

The Royal College of Surgeons of England

do hereby admit

Sir Henry S. Wellcome, LLD, FSA.

AN

HONORARY FELLOW

of the College.

As Witness our Common Seal this *Tenth* day of *March* 1932

President

Vice Presidents

Enrolled by *S. Forrest Cowell* Secretary

It is hereby certified that

Henry Solomon Wellcome Esq.

LL.D.

was on the 27th day of January admitted to

The Freedom

of

The Worshipful Society of the Art and Mystery of Apothecaries of the City of London

Honoris Causa

And his admission duly recorded in the books of the said Society

Master   Wardens   Clerk of the Society

Apothecaries Hall
1931

180 …Knighthood | **Above | Henry Solomon Wellcome, 1906 (head and shoulders). Oil painting by Hugh Goldwin Riviere.**

Above | The Grant of Arms of Sir Henry Wellcome. Henry Wellcome was created a Knight Batchelor by His Majesty King George V in the New Years Honours of 1932

On 18th February 1987, a memorial service for Sir Henry Wellcome was held in the crypt of St. Paul's Cathedral, London. A commemorative plaque was placed on the wall of the crypt. The Knights Bachelor chapel can also be found in the cathedral. The Chapel, also known as St. Martin's Chapel, is panelled in English oak. Here, two "elegant" cases contain registers recording the names of all Knights Bachelor from 1257 to date. In 2008 the chapel was dedicated by Her Majesty Queen Elizabeth II.

Bibliography

"Always read stuff that will make you look good if you die in the middle of it"
P. J. O'Rourke

Addison, Frank (1949) Jebel Moya. The Wellcome excavations in the Sudan. 2 vols. Oxford: Oxford University Press

Arnold, Ken, Olsen, Danielle (Eds.) (2003) Medicine man: the forgotten museum of Henry Wellcome. London: The British Museum Press

Boisseau, Tracey Jean (2004) White queen: May French-Sheldon and the imperial origins of American feminist identity. Bloomington: Indiana University Press

Fisher, R. (1978) Syrie Maugham. London: Duckworth

Greene, Graham (1936) Journey without maps. London: William Heinemann Ltd.

Hall, A. R., Bembridge, B. A. (1986) Physic and philanthropy; a history of the Wellcome Trust. Cambridge: Cambridge University Press

Hastings, Selina (2010) The secret lives of Somerset Maugham. London: Random House Inc.

James, Robert Rhodes (1994) Henry Wellcome. London: Hodder & Stoughton

Larson, Frances (2009) An infinity of things: How Sir Henry Wellcome collected the world. Oxford: Oxford University Press

Legrand, Jacques (1998) Chronicle of the 20th century. London: Longman

McKnight, Gerald (1980) The scandal of Syrie Maugham. London: W. H. Allen

Myers, Robin, Harris, Michael (Eds.) (1998) Medicine, mortality and the book trade. Folkestone: St. Paul's Biographies Ltd.

Ondaatje, Michael (1992) The English patient. London: Picador

The Oxford Dictionary of Quotations (1979) 3rd Ed. Bury St. Edmunds: Book Club Asssociates

Stanley, Henry M. (1890) Through the dark continent or the sources of the Nile around the great lakes of equatorial Africa and down the Livingstone river to the Atlantic ocean. London: Sampson Low, Marston, Searle & Rivington.

Stanley, Richard, Neame, Alan (1961) The exploration diaries of H. M. Stanley; now first published from the original manuscripts. London: William Kimber

Taylor, Sheila (2001) The moving metropolis; a history of London's transport since 1800. London: Laurence King

Theroux, Paul (2002) Dark star safari. London: Penguin

Turner, Helen (1980) Henry Wellcome: The man, his collection and his legacy. London: Heinemann Educational Books

Waugh, Evelyn (1930) Vile bodies. London: Chapman and Hall

Waugh, Evelyn (1945) Brideshead revisited. London: Chapman and Hall

Williams, Peter (2010) The story of the Wellcome Trust. Hindrigham: JJG Publishing

Image Below | Henry S. Wellcome in warrior costume with helmet 1885